Brian Fleming Research & Learning Library
Ministry of Education
Ministry of Training, Colleges & Universities
900 Bay St. 13th Floor, Mowat Block
Toronto, ON M7A 1L2

THE CONSUMER LEARNER

Emerging Expectations of a Customer Service Mentality in Post-Secondary Education

DR. GILLIAN SILVER AND DR. CHERYL LENTZ

The Consumer Learner: Emerging Expectations of a Customer Service Mentality in Post-Secondary Education
Education/Adult & Continuing Education $24.95

Pensiero Press
9065 Big Plantation Avenue
Las Vegas, NV 89143-5440 USA
info@consumerlearner.com
http://www.consumerlearner.com

All rights reserved. No part of this book may be reproduced or transmitted in any form or by any means, graphic, electronic or mechanical, including photocopying, recording, taping, Web distribution, or by any informational storage and retrieval system without written permission from the publisher except for the inclusion of brief quotations in a review or scholarly reference.

Copyright © 2012 by Pensiero Press

Library of Congress Control Number: 2011924558

Volume ISBNs: Hard Cover: 978-0-9828740-4-2
                E-book/PDF: 978-0-9828740-5-9
                Kindle and electronic versions available

Pensiero Press logo and cover design by Peri Poloni-Gabriel,
   Knockout Design (www.knockoutbooks.com)
Interior production by Gary A. Rosenberg
   (www.garyarosenberg.com)

Printed in the United States of America

10   9   8   7   6   5   4   3   2   1

Contents

Foreword, vii

Preface, xi

Acknowledgments, xiii

INTRODUCTION
The Emergence of a Transformational Paradigm Shift, 1

CHAPTER 1
The American Adult Learner Model in Review, 7

CHAPTER 2
Divergent Needs of the Adult Learner, 19

CHAPTER 3
Evolution of the Adult Learner Model, 29

CHAPTER 4
Student as Customer, 41

CHAPTER 5
Interpersonal Dimensions, 51

CHAPTER 6
Technology as a Tool
for Educational Transformation, 61

CHAPTER 7
Measures of Success and Outcomes, 73

CHAPTER 8
The Path of Least Resistance, 83

CHAPTER 9
Classroom Culture, 89

CONCLUSION
Transitioning Toward a Mutually Beneficial
Interpretation of Learning Consumption, 95

EPILOGUE
Stories From the Trenches, Contemporary Educational
Challenges and Practices, 105

References, 111

Index, 117

About the Authors, 119

*No problem can be solved by
the same consciousness that created it.
We need to see the world anew.*

—Albert Einstein

Foreword

OUR WORLD IS ONE OF RAPID CHANGE, and most people know that they must keep up with new technologies, skills, and learning generally. Within a generation, life-long learning, retooling skill sets, adaptive learning, and education for life have trumped the mind set of traditional classroom philosophies with its singular outcome of seeking a degree and a lifetime career. The pace of innovation in technology has transformed knowledge, and has made adult learning exciting, even ubiquitous.

Tracking changes in adult learning is captured well by the authors of *The Consumer Learner: Emerging Expectations of a Customer Service Mentality in Post-Secondary Education.* Dr. Gillian Silver and Dr. Cheryl Lentz present an analysis that tracks the transformation, and adds dimension to our understanding through the consideration of three vantage points of change—administrative, faculty, and student. It is the student vantage point; however, that is the most dynamic aspect of change in adult education. With their work experience, stresses in the home, and even grandparents needing to learn the technologies of their grandchildren, adult learners know they have to keep learning. And more and more, they want to set the goals and ground rules.

This book is really about the maturity and diverse interests of the adult learner: how they are motivated to learn; how they perceive faculty members as coaches and resources; and how they see education as a tool for their career goals, regardless of how frequently those goals may change. The adult student brings an understanding of the market place to education, and formulates plans and schedules to advance personal career objectives. They are the consumer of their learning, and they expect educational structures to respond.

Recognizing a shift in the learning paradigm, the authors detail a changing landscape and challenge the reader to understand and adapt with flexibility and feedback. From the beginning, the intention of the book is to initiate a dialogue about the new adult learning environment. Undoubtedly, in this transitioning environment, distinctive ideas and network-based sharing of ideas will emerge. For example, the authors provide a web site for comments, stories, and observations about the consumer learner to elicit comments from contributors from all areas of the learner-faculty-institution relationship.

In this emerging environment, community colleges are uniquely suited to respond to the consumer learner. The mission of the community college is student learning, whether it be for a one course, a certificate program or a degree. Market-responsive education and training is what many students today expect from their college or trade school, and community colleges are well positioned to deliver.

Foreword

The authors of *The Consumer Learner: Emerging Expectations of a Customer Service Mentality in Post-Secondary Education* thoughtfully share their perspectives and analysis of the adult learner today and invite us all to adapt to the change.

Dr. Mike Richards
President
College of Southern Nevada
http://csn.edu

Dr. Mike Richards is president of one of the largest community colleges in the United States. The institution has granted degrees to more than 25,000 students—from traditional age learners to those returning to the post-secondary environment for additional certifications and to launch new careers.

Preface

THE INTENTION OF THIS BOOK IS TO INITIATE a dialogue about the multi-faceted transformation of the higher education environment. Throughout the past two decades, the rise of the adult learning model has removed educational access barriers and enabled more individuals from diverse backgrounds—including women, minorities, full-time employees, and students returning to complete unfinished degrees—to experience intellectual growth and program achievement. Subsequently, certain variables have led to a cultural shift from a literature and conceptually centric focus to one in which students are becoming *consumer learners*. Within our work, this term symbolizes the diverse views of the adult education community and the process of seeking, evaluating, applying, and challenging knowledge.

Our purpose in presenting this work is to offer three unique perspectives, or vantage points, from which to consider the complex requirements of learners, the institutional demands for efficiency and cost-recovery, and the practice obligations of professional educators. Care has been taken to explore the environment in which we find ourselves as a result of both our teaching and student experiences. The intention is to do so with balance and fairness, rather than prejudice or from the sensibilities of only one of the three partners involved in the institution-student-educator partnership.

Throughout this book, we will return to these multiple lenses to create a holistic depiction of the evolution of higher education, and to conduct a review of key aspects of the transformation. Clearly all entities and individuals affiliated through the process of adult learning—the institutional administration, the faculty, and the student—bring valuable, and yet often incongruent, dimensions to this discussion.

We invite you to join us as we offer these open-ended perspectives for consideration by our colleagues within institutions of higher education and learning. Our desire is to understand what these factors, observations, and experiences mean to you the reader. Should you be willing, we invite you to share your opinions and expertise as we begin to contemplate what the historical context and the current forms of change might ultimately mean to the future of higher education.

Please contact us at info@consumerlearner.com to share your stories as we continue our work with *Epilogue: Stories From the Trenches, Contemporary Educational Challenges and Practices.* We look forward to your contributions of lived experiences as we examine how these separate yet inter-related components and discoveries integrate as we explore the larger question of the *consumer learner.*

Acknowledgments

THE AUTHORS WOULD LIKE TO ACKNOWLEDGE their husbands, administrators, faculty mentors, colleagues, and scores of adult learners who have served as points of inspiration throughout their professional and intellectual journeys. Thank you for challenging us to continuously excel.

INTRODUCTION

The Emergence of a Transformational Paradigm Shift

A DYNAMIC TRANSFORMATION HAS BEEN TAKING PLACE within the culture of post-secondary education that transcends the philosophy and structure of traditional 4-year, 2-year, and for-profit institutions. The myriad of changes are diversified and offer abundant opportunity for discussion. This evolution is quite distinctive from the educational climate either of us experienced during our time in our undergraduate, graduate, or doctoral experiences, and professional pursuits. It feels as if we are on the precipice of an enormous philosophical shift. This book strives to provide insight into the implications of the new setting being experienced by adult learners, administrators, faculty—and even the business community which benefits from the competencies cultivated by institutions of higher learning.

In our discussion with current educators and faculty, clear signals of change seem to have become apparent to many in the last 4 or 5 years. Although these indicators are not yet fully understood. It is vital to examine the pertinence of these indicators and the corresponding influence on administrative structure, faculty practice, learner outcomes, and the overall educational experience.

The purpose for this book is to provide a summative view of key considerations that helped to form the contemporary adult education arena. Further, reflective questions are extended to begin a dialogue in search of definitive answers. We strive to be objective and inclusive in our review, as the aim is to create meaning and to integrate discoveries. There have been numerous evolutionary developments and emerging perspectives that benefit educators by cultivating a more effective exchange in the classroom, and fulfilling student experience.

The process requires a brief historical journey that points to the embedded regard for cognitive and interpersonal growth found in the philosophies of the American education system. Stubblefield and Keane (1989) documented the influence of English culture in the colonial period of this nation, and how settlers "sought to establish a new society, a utopia, conserving the best of their heritage yet exploring opportunities previously denied them" (p. 27). As these authors noted, "improvement in all its forms, from intellectual to political and from social to economic, was implicit in their perceptions of the New World. The question thus arose as to whether adults could redress their inequalities and enhance their opportunities" (p. 27). The pertinence of this inquiry continues to be relevant in the 21st century, particularly because of the associated challenges of the continuing economic recession, and is, therefore, one of the themes addressed here.

Another significant observation presented in this volume is the unique transformation of the student/faculty relationship. In the early days of the collegiate structure in the United States, faculty positions were revered. Further, the process of education was considered a worthy aspiration that cultivated knowledge and deep examination of life's curiosities. Its pursuit was seen as critical to the evolution of American society, as the citizenry strove to contribute in distinctive, new ways to an expanding world. The professoriate was a well-regarded body which held final authority, both as subject matter experts and as the figurehead within the classroom. As such, those who earned entrance into the formal world of academia had achieved an assured level of control over the content, and the processes. The professoriate and administrators enacted a formal discipline; they held a nearly encompassing influence on the assessment of the educational activities and process.

While the content of the course was always intended for, and open to, discussion between the faculty and student, a level of respect was accorded the educator and maintained throughout the exchange. This position of authority and knowledge was never in question. This base of understanding was an outgrowth of the classical system shaped by Aristotle and others revered for their command of logic, and wide span of expertise. The interactive dialogue within the classroom could challenge facts and etymology, as well as assertions and conclusions; yet the relationship between faculty and student was honored, respected, and maintained. The educator was clearly the dominant intellectual force in the classroom and the student subordinate to the structure and ideals of the American collegiate educational system.

Somewhere in the last decade perhaps beginning as early as 2000, the balance in the educator relationship appears to have moved to a level that is more equal for all participants. The educator is now a resource, and the adult learner often drives—and demands—the classroom discourse. This transformation has growth from the initial presentation of Knowles' (1950, 1962,

1973, 1989) andragogy concept to his endorsement of the self-directed learner concept. Concurrently, this evolution is illustrated by Kolb's (1984) experiential learning theory (ELT), Speck's (1996) advocacy of blending adult learning theory with professional development activities, and York's (2000) view of action learning.

This transition often encompasses contradictory, but simultaneously similar, student practices in the quest to create a pertinent educational process that remains sufficiently challenging. A balance must be achieved that is acceptable, from the perspective of the educational community grounded in valid and reliable methods and materials. For example, older and returning adult learners are clearly intrigued by ideas yet less willing to accept textbook content as an ultimate source than the college-level students of yesteryear. The adult learner relies heavily instead on their own frame of personal and professional development as a lens through which to determine what is pertinent and immediately applicable.

The adult learner wishes to move ahead aggressively, to be efficient in the completion of their written papers, and successful on their exams. Information is rapidly accessed and evaluated. However, the very expediency of technology, and the reliance on often questionable content accessed through the World Wide Web that encourages students to view published material as immediately obsolete also causes a dilemma in the education of contemporary students. This interpretation of readily available background from often unverified sources is concerning as this technique is widespread in its depth, and does not account for the potential inaccuracy of easily found content. For adult learners, efficiency of learning means more time for work and family. For educators, shortcuts in research means compromised integrity in critical thinking and results.

The Emergence of a Transformational Paradigm Shift

The college educator also has come to be viewed as a resource, rather than the predominant originator of the ideas central to the course exploration. The evolution of this relationship has brought alterations in educational structure, orientation, delivery, performance expectations, and the assessment of student outcomes. The learner-centric focus is of enormous pertinence to us here, but we are also intrigued by the emergence of the student as not only the recipient of knowledge within the classroom, but how somewhere along this continuum, student and faculty communication has moved toward a more *transactional business* approach. This recognition of a paradigm shift, where students play a more dominant—and some say *dominating* role —in the educational process is taking root as early as in their formative schooling. For example, according to Arum and Roksa (2011) "students in K–12 and particularly in higher education increasingly became defined as 'consumers' [and] 'clients'" (p. 15). By the time these learners reach college, their concept of responsiveness may merge with the view of service to paying customers who have a choice of where they pursue degree acquisition. This transition in thinking changes interactions with the system, and in those who translate—and hopefully make relevant—the curriculum.

Instead of an exchange of knowledge and wisdom as a result of the experience, the contemporary student looks to the faculty as a means to an end—a marketable, immediately applicable degree. We have termed this individual the *consumer learner*, as he or she wishes to absorb information, put this information into use, and leverage the strength of the institution with whom they are affiliated. Time is of the essence, as education is now a pursuit of employment, promotion, or transition into a new career rather than merely a journey of intellectual expansion. A highly practical element is at play here, as the educational processes morphs from its traditional sensibilities to a contemporary partner in the delivery of education. According to Hames (2007), "Institutionalized learning has led to the fragmentation and perhaps irretrievable loss of human knowledge" (p. 12).

Both strengths and drawbacks are associated with this new view. Students are demanding educators who possess deep experience in industry as well as command of theory, concepts, and best practices. They want professors and associate faculty who can bridge the gap and translate complex ideas, to help learners make the knowledge their own. To some degree, students also want the process itself to be dynamic, as many feel entitled to expect entertainment, self-fulfillment, and self-satisfaction from the educational exchange. This process may generate more awareness, and engaged learners, as contributors to American industry. "Sociologists Walter Powell and Jason Owen-Smith have astutely observed that 'the commercialization of university-based knowledge signals the university's role as a driver of the economy'" (Arum & Roksa, 2011, p. 10). Consequently, a paradigm shift is taking place.

The collegiate faculty is no longer simply responsible for the expected course learning objectives, but must fulfill customer service expectations as well. Therein lies the quagmire—how do institutions continue to provide integrity programs while meeting market needs for employers, and providing viable and intriguing experiences for those who consume the material? We will provide insight into this dilemma by delving into the perspectives of administrators, students, and faculty in the chapters that lie ahead.

CHAPTER 1

The American Adult Learner Model in Review

MUCH EFFORT HAS BEEN INVESTED IN DEFINING the nature of the adult learner and, arguably, Malcolm Knowles (1950, 1962, 1973, 1989) has been one of the most powerful and enduring voices. In a business and academic career that spanned nearly five decades, he advanced the notion of the older learner as distinct from the child learner. Knowles (1989) readily acknowledged that as people age, their interests change and their motivations expand. As a result, educational delivery practices require continual modification as student interests do not naturally align with traditional lecture-style delivery. The term *andragogy* emerged as an expression of Knowles' (1989) views, and has been widely adopted as an approach to a philosophy that placed the learner in the center of the educational process.

As the literature progressed, the conclusion became clear; there was no singular, all-encompassing way to express the motivations and learning style preferences of the experienced adult. While pronounced commonalities could be identified, significant distinctions in interest, competency, and commitment also were present. Educators had no short-hand arsenal of practices upon which to rely. Nor was there a clear-cut way to consistently address the multi-faceted nature and diversity of their more engaged, and often deeply experienced, adult learners.

In the post-World War II generation of the 1950s, and the social awakening of the 1960s, a dramatic transformation was also occurring in higher education. Rather quickly, barriers (such as a male-centric student population and instructional ideology, and financial access restrictions) were being identified and removed to accommodate a wider array of adult learners. Concurrently, the emphasis shifted from mastery of historical foundations of concepts and theories to the immediacy of the content. Adults brought a quest for pertinence and relevancy to the classroom. Activities began to emphasize identifying and solving problems, and building a range of transferable skills. Analysis was still taking place, but its application was radically different.

The primary American education model was rooted in the elitist tradition of preparing the leaders of commerce and the clergy. As more students of advanced age, veterans, women, and minorities entered into college programs, it was predictable to assume change would not take hold in all educational environments with equal vigor. Traditionalists in the institutional arena likely saw the shifts occurring on simultaneous levels but initially resisted reform.

Whether this was primarily attributable to a romantic attachment to the standards and norms that had guided their development since the early days of the nation's public colleges or pure reluctance to amend rather than direct, the result was the same: administrators, for the large part, expected students to adapt. The colleges themselves were institutions, rooted in formality, norms, customs, and certain ways of performing. These institutions of higher learning would prevail with limited disruption to the staid processes of building curriculum, assembling programs, extending classes, teaching content, and assessing student outcomes. At first, learners complied, as they were few and the university and college system was strong. Adult learners were, essentially, limited in their influence against the protocols of deeply embedded institutional programming. Enrollment increases saw the emergence of new perspectives that would re-shape academic assumptions on the part of all involved.

Out of this turbulent time in which more adults sought education but challenged the often stodgy educational delivery system, grew a period of innovation. Nonconformists who understood marketing principles recognized there was a vast, eager population desiring the benefits of a college degree but that these individuals were dissatisfied with existing academic options. Holding the lion's share of classes during the daytime, presenting content through a predominant lecture modality, and using career academics who pontificated on the literature, were all seen as signals that the status quo—the traditional American higher education model—was on its way to obsolescence.

Emerging adult learners were less inclined to engage in residential studies, and they were not content to take one class a semester. These sociological elements and changes in orientation combined to make many 4-year state institutions undesirable places for the completion of a stalled degree, or the acquisition of new competencies. Community colleges such as Miami Dade (South Florida), Maricopa (metropolitan Phoenix) and Southern Nevada (Las Vegas and key rural communities) capitalized with a myriad of 2-year degrees and certifications intent on building technical skills. Out of necessity, other adult-oriented models began to take hold, notably John Sperling's University of Phoenix. This model incorporated practitioner educators who brought corporate backgrounds into the classroom and supplemented textbooks with illustrations of how business really works, and what strategies are needed for enduring success.

The business environment was clearly demanding a closer alignment of skills required in a globalized economy. Postsecondary education was no longer being seen as a lagging indicator, one that trailed the demands of the business world, but as a partner in a shift driven by the *consumer learner*. The adult scholar was now in charge, driving the demand for a cutting-edge academic product to serve their needs, with *the learner*—not the business environment—as its engineer.

Other early pioneers who applied this orientation to capture adult learners included the DeVry Institute of Technology (founded in 1931 which later emerged as the more well-known DeVry University), Kaplan Higher Education (previously the American Institute of Commerce and later Quest College), Corinthian Colleges (which operates Everest and WyoTech) and Strayer. Even administrators at historical Jesuit institutions such as Regis University saw the need to revamp curriculum to make content more digestible and relevant to working students who combined school with other life pursuits. Concurrently, there arose a shift in demand to a learner-centric focus. Now, the American adult could effectively select from diverse educational options to literally *consume* learning through a philosophy and delivery template aligned with their interests.

Traditional institutions, both public and private, did not initially accept the onslaught of new rivals and new thinking and delivery systems as welcome advancements in educational thought and process. These hallowed halls of academia challenged emerging new academic institutions as merely profit-oriented, uneven in quality and poorly matched to the caliber of formal educational models. While capitalizing on the curiosity of adult learners was highly attractive, adjusting to their requirements was inconvenient from the perspective of administration. Consequently, many pre-existing universities became entrenched, rather than adaptive.

It is often said that competition breeds excellence, and within the quickly growing field of higher education, adult learners could exercise a choice—with their tuition dollars. In the prosperous days of the 1980s, many older learners adjusted their schedules and returned to the college campus. An even larger number enrolled in community colleges, completed certifications, or joined emerging institutions which boasted the same accreditation as traditional universities but offered longer, less frequent or single-night delivery classes on compressed schedules. Adults sought the models that most effectively met their requirements, and benefitted from the numerous options. Growth was unparalleled. New programs and buildings were created on America's college campuses, and scores of nontraditional universities entered the scene.

Everyone was a winner as the United States Department of Education reports tracked an emerging population trend. The average age of college students slowly moved from 18 to 20, to 23 and beyond, and classrooms reached capacity levels. Demand seemed unquenched.

By the late 1990s, with the emergence of the Internet and the need to be proficient in a new global community, newer adult education models quickly gained advantage. It was here that students cultivated public speaking, research, and writing skills sought by industry.

Comprehension and knowledge was gained through hands-on experience and direct transfer, rather than through the comparatively more passive approach of auditory-based, non-participatory learning. Students were expected to demonstrate their growing level of understanding through direct application in written assignments and verbal analysis of complex scenarios, rather than rote memorization and repetition.

Students emerged from this experience with a stack of papers to show proficiency and knowledge in case analysis that made them better prepared to understand the full scope and scale of business problems. The pendulum was swinging so far in favor of the new model that administrators and faculty in the old system were required to consider radical change. If students would not, or could not, come to the campus, the campus would go to them.

Education became portable. The introduction of distance education and hybrid or blended courses that combined online and on-ground delivery resolved many original access issues. This transformation was not only logical, but necessary as in its most basic terms, form follows function.

Where once education was responsive to the needs of the marketplace, albeit 2–3 years behind, the *consumer learner* could not be assuaged and demanded the closing of this gap, perhaps even leading the charge for innovation to serve their needs. If adult learners were to support the demand for a dynamic new form of education, institutions of higher learner could no longer afford to wait. With the advancement of the Internet, replete with portable laptop computers, and electronic tools in their arsenal, the *consumer learner* saw education as a business exchange where they wanted their education in much the same way as they wanted their access to information—when and where it was required. The translation of the product meant education had become available—on demand and on the fly—

on trains, planes, buses, and subways; on cell phones, computer hybrids, and Ipads®.

The information age has exploded with emerging technologies and a corresponding change in consumption practices and expectations. The *consumer learner* began asking institutions of higher learning to serve their insatiable need for information and technology—where expectations evolved ahead of the ability of many institutions' abilities to keep up. The *concept* of the classroom was, and remains now, a dynamic setting, changing in ways never before imagined. This new paradigm is driven perhaps by the innovative demands of *the student as consumer*—in a transitional business exchange where supply must meet demand, and where new competitors emerge when existing models fail to perform to the expectations of the *buyers* (adult learners) of educational products.

Suitability of a degree product does not necessarily translate into deeper knowledge and personal productivity toward academic outcomes. "Students often embraced a 'credentialist-collegiate orientation' that focused on earning a degree with as little effort as possible" (Arum & Roksa, 2011, p. 70).

Current day students can now vote with their tuition dollars as well as their textbook dollars. This change in the influence structure forces compliance by institutions of higher learner and publishers to change delivery methods which adjusts the face of educational curriculum by default. The emergence of textbook rental options such as Course Smart is simply one example of many available adaptations.

There is, however, a fundamental problem. The hallowed halls of academia change slowly and many post-secondary institutions are finding the lessons of consumer-driven curriculum and program tough to respond to, let alone follow. With educational budgets shrinking and tuition levels increasing, the question is how to close the gap of the *consumer learner* as they demand their academic experiences keep pace with those of the emerging social networking phenomenon such as Facebook, Linked In, and Twitter.

By mid-2008, in the early days of the American recession, adults who had not previously recognized the value of investing in a degree to further their careers started to see the necessity of staying current as jobs were compressed and promotional opportunities declined. College became a pathway to legitimizing what was gained (a degree) and a means by which to secure continued pertinence in industry. Students sought expanded understanding and skills, along with convenient delivery methods through which to receive educational content. This transitional period brought a series of corresponding concerns, namely a worry that if degree acquisition became the motivator, was the process of learning compromised in the process? If educational units were *packaged* for fast progression, for example, was knowledge retention sacrificed?

Administrators, faculty, and students alike began wondering whether the results were legitimate and enduring. While learners appreciated interactive classes where action learning capitalized on small group activities, and facilitators engaged students in questions and reviews rather than hours and hours of lecture, what did students really know, understand, and have the capacity to apply? While diverse opinions exist on whether these areas can truly be measured and accessed, and some educators question whether old andragogical or pedagogical techniques still in use still work within these modern frameworks, the question of how to provide, and assess, a pertinent collegiate experience persist.

Even businesses contemplated the impact and potential benefits. Were graduates functionally prepared to perform on the job? Did they possess transferrable skills, such as enhanced language and mathematical competencies that would bring direct benefits such as increased efficiencies and profit to the enterprise? Did degree acquisition translate into critical thinking skills or did it merely represent an expensive piece of paper that brought with it expectations of promotional opportunities and higher compensation?

Vantage Point #1: Administrators

In recent decades, external environmental variables have demanded change. As much as institutions have been striving to keep pace—to continually extend pertinent curriculum, to make the nation well equipped to succeed—internal adjustments are complex and a national funding crisis makes challenges even more difficult to counter. While students increasingly request new modalities, interactive classes, portable education, and expansive electronic libraries with scores of databases, aging physical infrastructures require maintenance, accreditation programs require attention, and legislators demand program reductions as shrinking budgets become an ever-constant reality. Can the institution position the learner *first* with these current fiscal demands particularly in the middle of a recessionary crisis? Or does doing so place emphasis on priorities that, while vital, do not ensure institutional longevity?

Vantage Point #2: Faculty

One significant outgrowth of the rapid and dynamic changes in the American higher education landscape is that educators, particularly those who come into the classroom from the business arena, understand the diversity of contemporary adult learners. Students are of traditional and nontraditional age, starting out in industry or never-employed, re-careering and transitioning to new occupations and new industries, and veterans moving from the highly structured environment of the military to the corporate setting.

The average class increasingly consists of more women, first generation college students, and retirees. No section is like one taught before. No canned lectures make sense to all students, and the entire process of communication is still fraught with error, misconceptions, and multiple opinions. The very term *non-traditional learner* is a misnomer, as all adult learners are distinct and deserving of understanding. While there are many ways administrators strive to classify students, the educator is less concerned with grouping people by commonalities and more concerned with supporting their differences and reaching them as individuals.

Vantage Point #3: Students

The United States is a nation in which the entrepreneurial spirit thrives. Citizens exercise their right to be vocal on matters of interest, and are not complacent. The American educational system was established based on models that had their time and place and evolved to better serve a more encompassing set of expectations.

Today's students expect to be fully involved participants in their education, not passive recipients. If they meet the requirements (program design), a reward (the degree) is earned, and students deserve the option of many delivery forms (institutions) from which to select degrees that best suit their needs.

Perhaps this shift also changes the role of faculty where the learner expects faculty to be their coach as well as their educator, and guide through the curriculum material. Using a Rogerian (1995) approach (as cited in Stober & Grant, 2005), a cognitive coaching technique is applicable where the students may very well have the answers within them, where the role of the faculty is merely to draw out experience that is brought with them as part of the adult learner. This approach connects the cognitive process using constructivism to build on what the adult learner already knows. This is the benefit of the practitioner model where the faculty has both theoretical as well as practical experience that holds relevancy and meaning to help the student draw conclusions through the ideas of praxis—bringing theory and reality as close together as possible to enhance the overall experience for the learner. "Rather than focus on the parts of the system in isolation, systems theories focus much more on the relationships between parts" (Cavanagh as cited in Stober & Grant, 2006, p. 317). The student does not live in a vacuum, but in an increasingly expansive world which requires meaningful contributions.

SUMMARY

This chapter extended an understanding of the origins of the American post-secondary education system, and key factors contributing to its current evolution in philosophy, structure and practice. Noted in this discussion were several examples that addressed the essential nature of deliberately designing experiences that engage the adult learner and bring him or her directly into the center of the learning process. This theme will be interwoven in subsequent chapters, as the notion of the *consumer learner* becomes even more relevant. Faculty, administrators, and students are the three prongs of a dynamic intertwined relationship as higher education seeks to remain relevant and well-utilized.

The device of the vantage points serves to frame the perspectives of the individual partners in the educational process. The intention here is to incite curiosity—and potentially debate among the collegiate—so that empathy is gained and potential refinements are perhaps more easily identified.

CHAPTER 2

Divergent Needs of the Adult Learner

ADULTS AND CHILDREN CLEARLY DIFFER in their methods for acquiring and assigning meaning to information. While repetition is a mainstay of a youngster's intellectual development, adults prefer complex, multi-faceted ideas that require assessment, and may be solved in numerous ways. Adult learners are often intrigued by *the examination of the gray* and may be less comfortable with generalized, or even pre-scripted, answers. This variance in curiosity levels and the capacity to process ideas is of particular importance when considering the opportunity to do more than merely take in material but to make this material one's own and to potentially make improvements upon it.

Alexander Kapp is credited with coining the term *andragogy* as a reference to Plato's theory of education; however, Malcolm Knowles is most commonly acquainted with the reference point as he fully articulated the distinctions between learning in childhood and at a level of adult maturity. By focusing on the behavior and key characteristics of adult learners, Knowles (1990) holds that adults have psychologically transitioned into a state of self-concept and self-direction. If this theory is accepted as valid, educators must strive to provide learners with content that is not only of merit but of *pertinence and relevancy* (Brookfield, 1987, 1990).

On paper, this is a straight forward, sensible conclusion to embrace: educators must provide connections that are relevant and show the *what's-in-it-for-me* (WIFM) aspect inherent in all content. From a practical standpoint, however, the challenge is enormous. Consider, for example, that depending on institutional size and delivery methods, an average on-ground college classroom gathers a dozen to 100 individuals to study a subject that may not be of great personal or professional interest to the majority of those assembled. How are the principles of effective adult education—andragogy—successfully applied? How can precise learning outcomes be achieved with consistency and in a manner that satisfies student interests?

In his self-authored summary of these concepts, Knowles (1990) presents key assumptions that motivate learning and self-direction. He contends a need to know must exist, or examination of new ideas and options will not occur. Learners must possess an understanding of themselves or self-concept, have sufficient life experience so they can draw conclusions from new information, be ready to learn, and bring a motivated orientation to the learning situation (Knowles, 1990, p. 57). Andragogy demands from its practitioners a fluid temperament, and an ability to adapt to the students' unique requirements to capitalize on learning potential. Concurrently, however, the educator must be true to the content. He or she must strive to address concepts with clarity, underscoring the importance of ideas and connections to students who may be eager to focus exclusively on the *why* rationalizations and *what now* conclusions. This begs the question: at what point in the andragogical model process does educator allegiance to material prevail over adult learner preferences?

Brookfield (1987, 1990) provided a helpful alliance between understanding the nature of the adult and how he or she learns with addressing the functional accountabilities of building knowledge, retaining what is gained and recognizing the value of applied course content. In his work, *Becoming a Critically Reflective Teacher*, Brookfield (1995) stated that educators teach to change the world, but that teaching without reflection has limited meaning.

The serious process of assessing content cannot be compromised if learning is to be reflective. Nor, as Brookfield (1995) suggested, can the educator abdicate their official functions in the class. He or she holds responsibility for the progression of the content and for the decorum of the environment and is not on an equal footing with the student.

Brookfield (1995) addressed the challenge of teachers reared in the North American tradition of democracy and involvement as they strive to gain full participation in the learning process. He stated that this interest is often projected as an educator's commitment to present themselves as moral equals with their learners. Essentially, the dialogue proceeds much like this:

> I'm no different from you so treat me as your equal. Act as if I wasn't a teacher, but a friend. The fact that there's a temporary imbalance between us in terms of how much I know about this subject is really an accident. We're co-learners and co-teachers, you and I. (Brookfield, 1995)

The result is often a demonstration of inconsistency in the manner in which the learning process is presented. Brookfield attributed this, in part, to the reluctance on the part of both partners to dispense with "culturally learned habits of reliance on, or hostility towards, authority figures." Further he suggests changes do not arise without challenge or difficulty.

> Like it or not, in the strongly hierarchical culture of higher education, with its power imbalances and its clear demarcation of roles and boundaries, teachers cannot simply wish their influence away. No matter how much they might want it to be otherwise, and no matter how informal, friendly, and sincere towards students they might be in their declarations of "at one-ness," teachers *are* viewed as different, at least initially. (Brookfield, 1995)

Just as the professor considers the value of viewing the student as worthy of regard and powerful in the exchange of knowledge, the *consumer learner* considers the implications of fracturing such a time-honored perspective of the educator as expert, and may readily embrace the notion of the instructor as equal. Most often, the contemporary learner holds that he or she is the epicenter of the educational exchange. The individual may also wish to actively challenge the position of the educator, to demonstrate self-sufficiency and independent competency.

In turn, the educator may need to re-assert the functional necessity of a hierarchical structure in the classroom. He or she must simultaneously allow for the most full, integrative form of exchange possible, yet remain fully cognizant of their accountability to stay on point, ensuring that learners receive appropriate foundational support. Formal content should be inclusive of concepts, theories, and historical underpinnings, not easy-to-follow highlights. By encouraging *consumer learning*, educators stress the necessity and relevancy of ideas, as well as the critical thinking skills of assessing information for source credibility, validity, and reliability. The intention is to recognize the merit of ideas, to apply deep versus surface thinking, and to share new discoveries with others to suggest the interconnectedness of the process. By capitalizing on the enthusiasm and synergy cultivated within a learning group, the educator leverages the classroom experience.

In addition, the educator also looks to capitalize on the aggregate experience level of the class, particularly as the adult learner is far more advanced than the traditional 21- to 24-year-old from years past. Consequently, higher critical thinking and refractive thinking—skills beyond the conventional wisdom or boundaries—are expected (Lentz, 2008). The adult learner integrates the idea of praxis to bridge academic theory with their personal experiences for a richer academic classroom or curriculum experience.

Contemporary students tend to uniformly reject the traditional model of lecture versus the facilitative discussion which incorporates the facilitator as the interpreter. The educator exists in the role as translator to build a bridge from the self-sufficiency of the *consumer learner* to their next focal point of instruction. Communication theory substantiates this observation as the most effective way in which to make a point is to engage the recipient of the message—thereby creating a two-way flow of ideas—rather than encouraging passivity. *Preferring* is distinct, however, from the learner's obligation to *support* a more dynamic instructional style as this style requires attentiveness *and* participation. This is an area in which students may be hesitant to accept a larger role in guiding their own learning experience by asking and answering questions, enthusiastically fulfilling breakout group exercises, and drawing salient conclusions from one unit before moving on to new areas of content.

Could this be a reflection of the educator lacking a similar understanding of the desired outcomes? He or she may hold the desire that students will gain intellectually, as well as operationally, from the learning opportunities. But, conversely, students may be operating from a base of expectations gained in high school. They may have the experience of receiving information on one level, as the faculty lectures, and is primarily accountable for conveying understanding. In this model, the student does not have to be fully engaged, just committed to recording copious notes which are then reviewed and potentially memorized, for regurgitation on an examination or other classroom assessment.

For students new to the college setting or returning to the classroom after a lengthy absence, this long-held perspective from a former culture or generation may be hard to move beyond. Learners may not be entirely prepared to visualize the information through the filter of enlarged accountability or clearly view themselves as occupying a new role in the dynamic exchange of knowledge. Adult, nontraditional learners face several types of barriers to learning. Colvin (2006), Wiggam (2004), and others categorize these challenges as dispositional, institutional, and situational.

Educators facing a quiet, reticent audience that wants to be *carried* through the material may also find it easier to retreat into traditional lecture mode. It is because of this natural leaning on both sides of the educational partnership that the practitioner educator may have an edge over the traditional professor when incorporating adult learning philosophies. The educator who brings experiential frames to the content can create distinctive new associations between the theoretical and the practical. He or she can strengthen the student experience by building on integrative introspection and encouraging learners to make the knowledge their own. The goal of the educator becomes helping the student see *what is already there*. Further, a flexible practitioner should be able to easily maneuver between methodologies, retreating into formalized lecture when necessitated, and breaking into question-and-answer or a student-guided recap of salient points, when appropriate.

Vantage Point #1: Administrators

As the formal authority of the institution, administrators are comfortable holding the reins of influence. They direct and control, thereby implementing the structure and establishing the traditions of the hierarchy. Policies and procedures provide a uniformity that ensures consistency in decision-making, and enables continuity. Many traditional 4-year colleges and universities naturally align closely with bureaucratic business models and have numerous levels of aligned functions. This inherent philosophical design slows down the ability to recognize and harness societal change, and to effectively adapt to new demands from industry. Even andragogy-aligned deans and department heads understand that what takes place in the classroom is distinct from the realities of operating the overarching system. Modifications require a large groundswell of support, and careful logistical adjustments that often depend upon endorsement by regents/school boards, and key funding sources including legislative bodies. Institutional response may be slow. Subsequently, the pace at which decisions are made could discourage both students and faculty.

Vantage Point #2: Faculty

Educators are often empathetic and social individuals who enjoy people and the exchange of ideas. They appreciate intellectual discourse and are inspired by students who demonstrate an equal love for learning and who prosper and bloom within the classroom under the careful tutelage of a caring educator. Interactive learning means the practitioner has made a positive impact, and that participants are moving to a position of growth and independence—faculty are seeing the possibilities and are eager to transfer them to business and to life. While striving to inspire discussion and thoughtful consideration, the educator must concurrently manage the classroom, ensure that students are making ample progress collectively as well as individually, are in adherence with policy, and are gaining a certain competency level in the fundamentals of the subject regarding learning outcomes and expectations. Rigor for the learning process must not be compromised purely to enable students to have an active role in their own intellectual development.

Vantage Point #3: Students

In an increasingly competitive world, students may view education not as a *process* but a *tool*. Education is often a direct outcome of capacity and effort and, where possible, should be short, abbreviated, and efficient. Faculty have the obligation to provide valuable and immediately applicable information that is immediately relevant to learners' personal, emotional and professional needs. Presenting content that is out-of-date or not directly related to how an idea can be put to use is wasting student time.

Emerging expectations suggest that educators should bend to the students' interests, and not lecture on content that does not seem relevant to their current requirements. However, to actively broaden this view and identify new examples to highlight as concepts and theories are time-consuming, and there is rarely a clear strategic application. Further, this information may be seen as old and not relevant so the faculty must make stronger connections for the learners to see its merit. To sustain their curiosity educators must engage students on many levels to meet short attention spans, their expectations of entertainment, and the competitive advantage of outlets such as YouTube, Facebook, and Twitter.

SUMMARY

While commonly grouped by demographic or psychographic commonalities such as age or program interest, adult learners are enormously diverse and difficult to categorize. Students elect to pursue a college education or to return to campus for multiple reasons. Administrators and faculty, who are by nature inquisitive, may recognize that learning for learning's sake may not intrigue today's learner. The challenge of knowledge acquisition may have less market value among these individuals than was previously held in prior generations of post-secondary students, as significant external societal pressures—such as a rollercoaster economy—places greater importance on highlighting business practices that may elevate one's career. The educator may see this shift in content focus as a concession, but would be wise to assume a larger view. If private and public colleges and universities exist to build competencies, it only follows that programs, curriculum products, and educational practices must be adaptive. This philosophy will shape the conversation that follows, as a brief historical retrospective illustrates the value of a responsive system that builds intellect and competency.

CHAPTER 3

Evolution of the Adult Learner Model

NO SINGULAR THEORETICAL FOUNDATION clearly or completely expresses a concept but when combined, the ideas grow in importance as each layer accentuates and builds meaning for the next. This conclusion follows true for the complex, ever-evolving area of adult education. Beder (1989) underscored, "Clearly purposes and philosophies are interrelated. Yet, they are also conceptually distinct" (p. 37). He addressed how arguments can be made for philosophy influencing practice, and how "the field's development in North America . . . has developed from purpose, because adult education has been more affected by the social function it serves than by the thought systems associated with it" (p. 38). Facilitating any form of transition in a dynamic setting requires increased knowledge—the gift educators hope to bestow upon their learners.

Beder (1989) echoed Hart's (1927) notion that "as values, attitudes, and beliefs change, so do social role expectations. As role expectations change, so must the behavior of adults change" (p. 39). Educators enable the adult learner to harness the possibilities of growth and to recognize—and apply—new avenues of intellectual and experiential discoveries. Institutional leaders must, therefore, also be flexible in their capacity to respond to developing industry demands. This approach will ensure that programs extend pertinent, meaningful content. Drawing from Beder's commentary, adaptation of both philosophy and practice is essential for today's college and university systems to best serve its beneficiary populations with regard to their emerging expectations of the collegiate experience.

As noted in the Introduction, the United States' system of higher education was modeled on the universities of Great Britain. Originally, post-secondary education was available only to those of privileged backgrounds, individuals entering the clergy, and those destined for industry leadership positions. Later experiences were expanded to include those who would serve in medicine, agriculture, and other emerging professions. The system was designed for those with certain sociological advantages; education was not a pursuit generally open to women or to minorities. (There were some exceptions such as the inclusion of John Sassamon, a Native American who worked on translation of the Bible, and the achievement of a Middlebury College degree in 1823 by Alexander Lucius Twilight, an African American).

Educational programs were also primary designed for the young—or what become known as the *traditional* learner. The only aged who benefitted were those who were already part of the process and who continued to study, work, and publish as part of the academic community. Hemricus College was created in 1611 but not chartered with degree-granting abilities until the creation of the United States in 1776. Therefore, Harvard University established by the Puritans as a colonial college, and founded in 1636, is considered the oldest institution of higher

Evolution of the Adult Learner Model

learning in the United States. Brubacher and Rudy (2004) indicated that while Yale began with only 36 students in 1710, reaching a peak of 338 in 1770, Harvard held 123 students in 1710 and 413 in 1770. "These were tiny provincial schools, often consisting of a president and one or two tutors. During the whole of the seventeenth century less than 600 persons attended" (Rudy, 2004, p. 22).

Granted the graduating classes of that era were tiny, they nevertheless comprised the intellectual and political elite of English America. The influence of this select group, and through it, of the colonial college itself percolated down to the mass of the population from the legislative assembly, the pulpit, the law court, the mercantile house, and the school. (Burbacher & Rudy, 2004, p. 22)

In 1837, the Institute for Colored Youth—now Cheyney University—was established. By 1869, Howard University opened the first black School of Law, with a concerted emphasis on supporting the needs of newly freed slaves. The Bellevue Hospital School of Nursing was established in New York City in 1873.

The foundation of the colonial American college built a structure "concerned primarily with training a special elite for community leadership. To these fundamental policies, this foundation held steadfastly and without essential change for nearly 200 years" (Burbacher & Rudy, 2004, p. 23).

Single-gender schools, such as Little Girls' School in North Carolina (later Salem College) which made its debut in 1772, were seen as finishing schools to teach young ladies manners and how to entertain. Academic content was limited to literature. In 1881, the institution now known as Spelman College was created and described as the first traditionally black woman's college, Atlanta Baptist Female Seminary. However, commonly acknowledged, it was not until 1883 when Stephens College (formerly the Columbia Female Academy) expanded the range of curriculum available to women. In addition to English grammar, studies included moral philosophy, algebra and celestial geography. By 1944, Stephens introduced the first aviation program for women, and prepared women to serve their nation in World War II.

Currently, the post-secondary trend is high levels of enrollment among nontraditional adult learners who may be returning to college after a period of substantial absence (Fiddler, Marienau, & Whitaker, 2006). Voorhees and Lingfelter (2003) and many others have defined these individuals as in their mid 20s and above, and returning to or now initiating college programs. This description is in sync with the U.S. Department of Education (NCEWS, 1999), which considers adult learners as those individuals engaged in some form of "instruction or educational activity to acquire the knowledge, information and skills necessary to succeed in the workforce, learn basic skills, earn credentials or otherwise enrich their lives" (U.S. Department of Education, 2011, Educational Statistics).

Through structures such as financial aid programs and the GI Bill, active and retired military veterans, along with first generation students, were provided the opportunity to pursue baccalaureate degrees. The Post 9/11 GI Bills are portable, which allows the transfer of benefits from the military member to their spouse or to their children. These changes further increase educational reach.

The American promise of educational access was realized with the introduction of new, for-profit institutions in the 1980s. It was here, in a distinctive new setting that placed merit on the direct application of ideas, that learners found a new model for educational consumption. Their achievements in the work setting, and subsequent capacity to identify direct points of transfer, meant more than performance on standardized academic instruments. Modifications in instructional methodology became more widespread in their use, and in some enterprising nontraditional universities tests were frequently used for reinforcement, not as the primary method of evaluating the understanding and retention of information.

By 2005, distance learning reached 2.5 million American students (U.S. Department of Education, 2005). In comparison, in just two and a half decades, the U.S. Department of Educational National Center for Education Statistics reported 12.3 million individual course enrollments in distance education courses (2008). Competency in the topics, terminology, concepts and theories were strategically demonstrated in extensive—and numerous—written assignments. Verbal proficiency was assessed through professional-standard presentations and mastery of software programs such as PowerPoint, and the technology infrastructure used to support their delivery.

Andragogy evolved to speak to the various ways of learning, and to the various learning styles and forms of intelligence identified by Gardner (1983, 1991, 1993, 1995). Goleman's (1995, 1998, 2005) notion of emotional intelligence was continually examined as students were asked to consider the consequences of selecting among alternatives, to uphold the obligation to make ethically sound decisions, and to contemplate the impact of their practice on business and on people.

Post-secondary institutions of higher learning focused extraordinary attention on curriculum integrity. Faculty were no longer the primary shapers of the content and context of the course. The variances from class-to-class based on instructional competency and articulation ability were made less extreme. This new approach introduced specific, measurable outcomes that synced with the sensibilities of industry, and echoed the popularized training model that spoke to highly designed learning units and resonated with industry leaders who desired more competent employees. Curriculum designers became actively engaged in the facilitation of constructs, creating a structured alignment of ideas, activities, and assignments.

As defined by Sperling in the early 1980s, the purpose of higher education was to establish a consistent base of comprehension and command of the material. Separate units of study could build upon prior learning experiences, and be provided in a sequential and linear fashion. Courses were linked to achieve program objectives, and to bridge between what was known and what was to be gained in the next learning experience. Program integrity was, therefore, enhanced as educators could capitalize, via the textbook, student content expertise, and the experiential framework learners brought to the class. The focus on the portability and immediate transferability of content enabled the *consumer learner* to transition from one academic endeavor to the next, and to leverage what was gained throughout the program of study.

In the process, the learner gained a certain level of literacy in the language, conditions, impacts, and value of business. Education became pertinent, and inspirational to the active adult who juggled the multiple stresses of life, home, and work obligations. Learning assumed a new prominence, as a result of the transactional means to an end. This process was considered viable if it met the self interest or the what-is-in-it-for-me (WIFM) mentality of the learner. This new view of the exchange process essentially conveyed the idea 'I'm interested as long as I can see the light at the end of a tunnel.' Educators were expected to respond accordingly, to motivate the student forward toward the achievement of the ultimate objective: degree attainment. The challenge to this new viewpoint was making the student recognize the viable linkages that served practical—yet academically sound—outcomes, and to thereby encourage the need to put forth an adequate level of effort.

Several years into the 21st century, students increasingly demonstrate the competence to *consume* ideas. The focus has shifted from memorization and regurgitation of content to the use of newly formed conclusions and competencies. The premise of the new adult learner—the *consumer learners*—is that adults are uniquely qualified to capitalize on the high ideals of the process itself to translate their own significant interpretations.

Robinson (1994) spoke to the merit of enabling students to reach their own conclusions regarding the material under study. He explained that "learning is not passive absorption, but an active process of translating new knowledge, insights, skills and values into one's conduct" (p. 3). As a result of this definition of the learning *process*, the *consumer learner* recognizes in him or herself many specific and unique characteristics that will shape the educational journey.

The adult learner can then be more concretely defined as one whom:

- wants to learn regardless of age
- is pragmatic in their learning to apply their learning to present situations
- [has] their own personal goals and objectives
- [has] a rich background of experience
- [is] motivated to learn based on a combination of external and internal forces

- [is] better motivated to learn when they are actively involved in the learning process. (Robinson, 1994, p. 2)

    These elements combine to form the *consumer learner,* an individual who is a wholly integrated component of their educational experience. This adult benefits from the Socratic Method of instruction, which involves constantly asking questions to challenge assumptions, bias, and perception. The approach familiarizes the student with his or her own capacity to challenge themselves and to bend thought—to scrutinize and to accept conclusions that appear to hold merit when weighed against experience and the demands of a given scenario.

    Through the pursuit and consideration of academic core principles and philosophies, the individual evolves into a more productive member of society. "They learn that the search for truth begins internally with asking the right questions which leads perhaps to the right or most appropriate answers" (Lentz, 2009a, para. 4). The enduring value of Socratic questioning is that this technique provides for disciplined questioning that can be used to pursue thought in many directions and for many purposes, including: to explore complex ideas, to reach the truth of things, to identify issues and problems, to uncover assumptions, to analyze concepts, to distinguish what is known from what is not yet understood, and to follow out logical implications of thought (Paul & Elder, 2006, p. 2).

    This transition of the continuum of dependency is similar to conventional wisdom with the idea of Knox (2009) and others with regard to praxis—bringing theory closer to proficiency and performance. As learning unfolds, the adult learner requires *guidance,* not firm instruction, and the ability to test out new ideas to navigate the gap between what *they know* to integrate with what they are *learning.*

Evolution of the Adult Learner Model

The foundational premise of the adult learner is paramount to the strategy of instruction as part of the educational process. Faculty must continue to meet and engage the adult learner *on his or her terms*. By more firmly understanding the definition of an adult learner, the faculty and academic institutions can more effectively employ strategies to meet these unique and specific needs for a more successful outcome.

The role of the contemporary American educator is not to give the student the right answer as there are no absolutes. By enabling them to understand that there are *many* possible conclusions, learners not only consume knowledge, they are empowered to apply what they have gained with proficiency. The instructor challenges understanding, stretches the realm of what is familiar, and in doing so, facilitates students who find their right answers through a legitimate process of critical and refractive thinking (Lentz, 2009a). The educator is present as a cheerleader to encourage, debate, and applaud contributions that motivate contemplation. He or she is there to assist the learner in embracing full participation. The concept of voting to fulfill one's civic duty is a relevant example. It is not the faculty member's role to tell a student for whom to cast their ballot, merely to encourage participation in this process.

Students do not like this lack of finite answers as they have been conditioned to expect a black or white response. They are uncomfortable with ambiguity. Further, adult learners are reluctant to accept that they alone are accountable for their performance in an academic program and for their transfer of those formalized outcomes into business settings. The educator bridges the gap between the expected and potential achievements, guiding student self-discovery and reflection. Through this operationalized change, a student moves from being *co*dependent, to being *inter*dependent with the ultimate goal of making them *in*dependent. In this transformation of *consuming learning,* the adult learner becomes capable of expanding knowledge and making their discoveries pertinent to industry dilemmas. Problem identification and resolution competencies emerge, and the individual then seeks to demonstrate their understanding and creativity. The evolution to consumer learning then becomes realized. The student becomes more engaged, leveraging their operational curiosity about how ideas transfer, and their quest for self-improvement to achieve the degree they cherish. In the process, the individual moves through the stages of co-dependency to interdependency. Lastly, the student emerges into independency with an enriched level of understanding and capability.

Vantage Point #1: Administrators

The American education system exists to serve all qualified learners. Certain measures, such as standardized academic testing (SATs) and performance indicators including grade point average (GPAs) are required to ensure learners are prepared to succeed, and are making ample progress in degree programs. Student success if further supported by making tutoring, English as a second language, and other services available to learners who wish to avail themselves of these opportunities. Colleges and universities do maintain the privilege of assessment, and students must earn a degree through demonstrated proficiencies. Factors such as student effort and educational progress require more precise measurement when the learner participates in a course by distance rather than in on ground, direct contact classrooms.

In addition to academic performance and upholding the rigor of educational activities, administrators also question the long-term impact of online programs on enrollment, suggests

Miller and Schiffman (2006). Further, providing content in a theoretical frame that works in a virtual environment poses challenges (Miller & Schiffman, 2006; Geith, Schiffnab, & Vignare, 2005). For technological change to succeed, adjustments in educational practices, curriculum design, and even disposition, will be essential to ensure that knowledge acquisition remains the first priority of any post-secondary institution.

Vantage Point #2: Faculty

Many ways of learning exist and significant research has demonstrated that individuals have different styles for processing information. By varying methodology and instructional practices, educators encourage learners to become actively engaged. The ultimate objective is always competency in the terminology, principles, and approaches of the field under study, so evaluation of student performance is essential. When a student passes a course, he or she should be, ideally, well-prepared to achieve in the next course in the program sequence.

Vantage Point #3: Students

Educators often get caught up in the rigor and importance of learning. In the process, emphasis is placed on topics that are trivial, old, or not that are of great importance to business today. Education is expensive and students have a right to earn high grades and should not be subjected to overly heavy amounts of testing or writing that does not transfer into skills employers value. If the student is the customer, his or her perspective must have a larger influence on the selection of content and how knowledge is taught. Quite simply, students want to have more of a voice in the process.

SUMMARY

This chapter briefly examined the remarkable evolution of the American post-secondary environment. As demonstrated by the increasingly expansive scope of collegiate programming, adult education principles have realized and enhanced opportunities for diverse populations, intellectual interest, and professional focus areas. The contemporary environment easily encompasses a student-centered focus. Slowly, the consumption of learning is being viewed from an adaptive viewpoint where the institution, faculty, and individuals adjust to changing expectations. Potentially, the shift results in the integration of applicable discoveries adding a new dimension to the notion of knowledge acquisition and—more important—transfer.

CHAPTER 4

Student as Customer

THE NOTION OF EDUCATIONAL CONSUMPTION is intriguing to ponder, particularly in the current-day environment of flux. No one would challenge the level of fluidity successfully modeled by the nation's institutions of higher learning in the past two decades. Adaptations include the progression, on most campuses, from the traditional 16-week delivery cycle to compressed schedules consisting of 8-week, 6-week, and 5-week classes. This includes the movement from twice-weekly meetings to three or four-hours once a week, and from on-ground and in-person classes to the introduction of distance education sessions to include the online modality.

Colleges and university sites have heeded the call of state regulators and Wall Street (the for-profit models) as the demand for demonstrated performance has intensified. Public post-secondary systems were directly challenged to up the ante as new private institutions efficiently entered (and some say) took command of the market. Curriculum content was modified to place greater emphasis on immediately transferable skills.

Subsequently, focusing on theoretical and conceptual foundations became a secondary concern.

The sheer impact of nontraditional students (older, re-careering, or returning-to-college learners) meant that most individuals were concurrently working while going to school. Many experienced tremendous time poverty as they were accountable for young families and, frequently, attending to the needs of aging parents. Degree or certificate attainment became one of many simultaneous demands on the adult student as they juggled a strenuous schedule and increased financial pressures. Subsequently, the demand of the academic process became longer, even with intensified and compressed delivery systems.

While the simultaneous reconfigurations and institutional resiliency served as a testament to their ability to respond proficiently, new challenges started to emerge. A willingness to evolve was only one dimension of the necessary adjustments. Post-secondary educators began reporting that students were exhibiting new behavioral dimensions. Attention spans seemed shorter in exhausted adults. Resistance to information viewed as non-essential by learners was voiced boldly without hesitation. Students demanded to know *why* content was relevant, and often rejected the establishment of a theoretical base as they were anxious for direct conclusions.

Students wanted concrete direct answers handed to them. Increasingly, learners expressed dissatisfaction with theoretical discussions and activities; instead they demanded case studies and other forms of practical inquiry requiring personal analysis and interpretation. The faculty members were pressed to make adjustments that ensured every element of the learning experience was relevant. Heidelberg (2008) documented the convergence of an *edutainment* movement where there is less use for the classical professoriate model and a blended delivery *zone* of entertainment and education. Students, challenged by massive amounts of preparation (reading, along with individual and group assignments), sought amusement when convened for class.

Adult learners desire technology-based delivery methods: stylishly designed PowerPoints, real-time Internet searches, videos, and forays into You-Tube postings. Rather quickly, the demand for digestible education that could be *consumed* by learners became an eye-opening call for action. Educators lamented the loss of substance and the potential sacrifice of content as complex ideas were broken down to the most common denominator.

Administrators spoke to the requirements of external accrediting bodies to validate degree programs, and the necessity of an outcome-based approach. The business community met with administrators to request more accessible tuition rates and more industry-specific material. Although the concurrently emerging shifts in focus were pronounced and multi-faceted, perhaps the largest philosophical transformation of all was creeping into view. The higher education area was evolving into a *provider* with a business market transaction mentality. The result of this transformation: a student-as-customer disposition.

Did the mindset among learners emerge from the application of a business model to the *consumer* of education? Was this change in mindset a reflection of a stressed-out populace surviving in an increasingly complex, competitive society in which the Americans brain-trust no longer prevailed? Did reduced attention spans and boredom serve as contributing elements? An absence in the mainstream literature exits to postulate on the most dominant reason, but experiential associations abound.

Demographic and psychographic indicators point to an aging society, with the largest amount of population growth occurring in the United States being recorded in the states west of the Mississippi in the lower 48: Arizona, Nevada, California, Utah, Colorado, and Washington (Case & Alward, 1997; U.S. Census, 2010). As individuals recognized that time is finite, expectations are altered. Further, post-secondary institutions in these geographic areas must adapt to the life-long learning expectations and service requirements of these older students.

The dramatic effects of a period of corporate compression, (middle-management downsizing), creation of multi-national conglomerates, followed by arguably the greatest economic downturn since the Depression, meant that stable, well-compensated positions with benefits were suddenly a hot commodity.

Employers, under the guide of efficiency management, leveraged the opportunities to eliminate full-time jobs. Part-time, on-call, temporary duty roles increasingly became the norm.

Rationalizing these conclusions could be accepted by administrators, faculty, and students alike, but it was the resulting classroom conduct modifications that symbolized a shift. Relationships among the three collaborative partners were challenged by a question of whether empowered *buyers* of education—these new consumers—would reliably achieve academic standards or challenge their veracity.

Vantage Point #1: Administrators

Education is about the pursuit of knowledge, but increasingly institutions must operate with a return on investment focus. This *transactional business* approach was emerging concurrently as education lost its value as a mechanism for knowledge transfer. Instead, the process of educational delivery is emerging as a true business model with a profit-driven focus. With budgets being slashed, sustainability of the academic institutions is being challenged. Can post-secondary institutions survive with current models? Or will they fail the test of adaptation? Has the goal for education evolved from classroom learning objectives to coaching to profit driven results and efficiency? Or, is the overarching directive in times of funding pressure shifting to economies of scale achievements?

Administrators are, therefore, charged with two concurrent requirements. These demands are intended to ensure the institutional mission by building an educated populace to support industry, while producing profitable programs that emulate lean management principles and tight cost control.

Student choice in the marketplace, is this a competitive advantage? For-profit institutions are taking to the airwaves of TV, radio, and social media to advertise and compete for tuition dollars. In the process of building institutional branding and program visibility, has education become commercialized? Instead of underscoring the importance of college at the high school level via the traditional academic pathways of guidance counselors and administrators, post-secondary institutions are using a consumer-centric marketing focus similar to the mass media channels used to advertise new homes for sale or investment opportunities. Has the heated marketing to generate tuition dollars raised the competitive bar to a new level? Is this a wise approach? Should the concentration be on reaching desirable numbers in the classroom versus recruiting appropriately qualified prospective students as future minds to educate?

Vantage Point #2: Faculty

Educators are caught in a bizarre conundrum and being pulled simultaneously by both administrators and students. Many faculty are starting to question if struggling institutions, driven by a profit motive, are acquiescing to this incentive to please as a means to retain students not as adult learners but as sources of income. Concurrently, faculty report the emerging demand by students is much like a business exchange. Students desire a level of entertainment in their contact hours, which evolves the professor into a customer service agent. Students expect to like their faculty, to be pleased by their faculty, and to demand customer satisfaction of their investment of tuition dollars much in the way one would buy a hamburger or a sports car. Adult learners insist upon a quality experience. Education has been reduced to a business *transaction* instead of an intellectual exchange of scholarly premise or theory discussion.

As part of a faculty's evaluation, instead of how well a faculty presents materials in the classroom, of how students achieve or exceed measureable learning outcomes. Increasingly, there is an additional element to consider: faculty must be popular among the learners. This shift from viewing the educator as a content expert translates into a factor of whether a faculty has met all of a student's social expectations as part of the educational experience. Further, the administration takes these end-of-course satisfaction scores into consideration when offering future contracts. This is of particular interest to part-time or adjunct faculty. Many report enhanced pressure to satisfy learners' interpersonal preferences and sense of what level of work, is *manageable,* rather than *challenging.*

Somewhere in this process, the educator has been asked to meet a customer service expectation in the mind of the student. The professor is no longer revered for their depth of scholarly knowledge and andragogical skill. Instead, the educator is now at the subjective mercy of an assessment that evaluates how well they pleased the personal and entertainment interests of their

Student as Customer

students, as opposed to learning objectives, curriculum agendas, and demonstration of learned course skills and theory. When did this paradigm shift from educator to customer service agent begin? Is this a positive or natural direction in which the relationship should evolve?

As the academic institute's representatives with *their feet on the ground*, faculty offer the most identifiable touch point in the student experience. Clearly, faculty provide the bulk of the direct educational exchange through interpretation of the essential core competencies to be gained in the course, delivery of the salient ideas and assignment instructions, and assessment of learner outcomes. Interpersonally, the educator's disposition shapes the student's view of the subject matter and its complexity. The professor holds within his or her classroom management strategies the ability to foster dynamic dialogue or to make potentially compelling content invigorating and pertinent, rather than flat, and nontransferable. In an emerging *consumer learner* environment, the faculty member can engage and direct understanding. They can reinforce the choice of the institution as a good fit, and can demonstrate how diligently student interests are supported. By placing continual emphasis on quality, post-secondary educators can provide a base of knowledge that is compelling, attractive, and pertinent.

Vantage Point #3: Students

The student views the faculty/student relationship as one of a transactional exchange. This perspective suggests inquiry; has the student received an adequate return on their investment (ROI) in terms of time, financial investment, social experience and relevance? Adult learners who might otherwise have seen the educational process as vital, stimulating and life-altering have had become pragmatic. College has a price—a steep one at that—time, energy, and challenging tuition and fees. In a free-enterprise system of many options a natural outgrowth was the view that money was exchanged—rather than invested—in an educational product. The process, the personal evolution the individual had the capacity to experience is becoming subservient to the end goal: a formal piece of paper documenting degree completion.

Contemporary students look to the process of obtaining this degree as one of social compliance. Has the professor met their interpersonal comfort goals? Has the professor become the personal and charming face of education as a spokesperson might be rated? When did the social experience circumvent or subjugate the higher purpose of learning?

As the cost of a college education escalates, students and parents alike are weighing the merits of a multiple-year investment that may generate a $35,000 (Baccalaureate) to six-figure (Masters) debt (The College Board Policy Center, 2011). The economics of higher education, and the often complex nature of loan structures, makes the decision to pursue a degree increasingly complex. Coupled with the recession and extensive level of job compression that continues to be experienced by the nation, students are evaluating the opportunities of college against the financial return of acquiring a degree and, ideally, the acquisition of a higher compensated position following graduation. This question of value doesn't dissipate once enrolled. Learners continue to weigh their interest in the subject matter, their ability to succeed, and the overall opinion of the educational experience against the expense.

For some, the notion of the *consumer leaner* is concentrated here—on the cost of education. Students may conclude they are engaged in a purchase, and adopt an expectation that coursework will be limited and easy to complete, and satisfaction is guaranteed. This vantage point frequently contradicts the administrative position that education involves rigor. The prevailing faculty view that there is a natural variance in learner performance and that a grade of an 'A' is earned, not awarded or up for negotiation.

SUMMARY

When external variables such as stable employment and professional advancement appear compromised, it becomes necessary to view post-secondary education from the perspective of a consumer mentality. The return on investment (ROI quotient) must be persuasive for the adult learner to make the commitment to a degree program. Student must have confidence in the curriculum and the instruction and view the experience as meritorious in light of the complex purchase decision.

This chapter encompassed the transformational dispositions toward education. Of all of the ideas expressed, the most crucial to consider is that educational integrity must not be compromised even when powerful market pressures favor the consumer. Students must accept that commitment, complexity and assessment of achievement are large components of the journey toward knowledge acquisition. It is crucial to leverage a deep understanding of the material if that knowledge is to be applicable in life and in work.

CHAPTER 5

Interpersonal Dimensions

ADMINISTRATIVE USE OF PART-TIME FACULTY is intended as a cost control strategy to better align the academic institution with a lean operating budget. Further, incorporation of working professionals as affiliate instructors provides the college or university with a strong experiential dimension as part of the student learning process. For the specific purpose of this chapter, the commonly used terms *part-time* or *adjunct* refer to all affiliate or associate faculty—those individuals who are not contracted on a full-time basis as instructors or professors. While these individuals provide more transferable insight than the teaching assistants commonly used in large universities, the nature of the relationship may be tenuous and based exclusively on institutional need. This arrangement is a challenge for all partners in the triad—administrators, faculty, and students. What is the level of continuing investment in the caliber of instruction if increasing numbers of adjunct faculty are used as a supplemental resource? Does the balance between part-time and full-time educators compromise the quality of the instructional experience? Does this quest for financial savings impact the performance of students by either increasing their continuity in enrollment or even their level of program completion?

ALIGNMENT OF INTERESTS RATHER THAN COMPETITION

In a time when economics shape institutional decision-making, are administrators appropriately applying intellect and experience in the classroom? Is the trend toward a greater reliance on part-time faculty producing positive impacts on the process of learning or is this perhaps merely a compromise? This part-time faculty model is increasingly surrounded by debate as capable, proven educators seek diversified employment opportunities to cover their bills (including the high cost of their own Master's and Doctorate degrees). Does reliance on generally less expensive part-time educators serve the institution's overall best interest or primarily its financial needs? Does a move to a part-time model provide for appropriate financial recognition of the practitioner educator's pertinent contribution to curriculum?

The faculty perspective is that in these need-based relationships, there are vulnerable and inconsistent patterns to address. This is due partially to a structure in which faculty compensation is based on a class taught. In the business realm, this would be called a pay-for-performance model or *task performance*. Classroom contracts are a package deal, where some universities pay by the student or by the class. The relationship exists, with no benefits or guarantee of continual employment, and are often described by faculty as tenuous.

The partnership with administration that assigns the classes is, at best, conflicted, and based on interpretation of learner *satisfaction* versus outcome-based performance. Consequently, this tug-of-war lends credence to the emergence of the *consumer learner* and a customer service-driven mentality. This evolution constitutes a challenge throughout the entire educational system, with particular impact on the adult learner. Matching credentialed personnel to a one-time course, rather than cultivating faculty to own, as well as continuously develop and refine the content, effectively comprises the integrity of the educational process as well as the overall student experience.

An associated potential compromise is that the instability of moving in and out of the academic system may weaken the assessment of faculty results across the spectrum of a degree program. While the educator's obligation is to review and rate student work, when students rate faculty performance and only the most popular adjuncts (as determined by high-scoring end-of-course evaluations) secure future teaching assignments, students may reward faculty who *give* grades rather than hold students accountable to *work* for high marks. Part-time educators who have the opinion that learners may underperform and expect a grade higher than performance warrants could potentially find that rejecting the notion of student entitlement results in poor evaluations and lost teaching contracts.

Another perspective to consider is whether the full-time faculty member and the adjunct alike have the time to remain alert to current developments in their respective disciplines or areas of expertise that make their classroom comments timely and pertinent. Is the focus on creating transferability of what is gained into business via future graduates? Or, instead, is the concentration placed on successful completion of the course, as indicated perhaps by high retention and strong grade point averages? It is crucial for educators to recognize that content in teaching is meant to be *used* for learning rather than *covered* (for testing).

Strong educators place importance on how ideas instill enthusiasm in students and spark curiosity. Faculty strive for currency in interpretations beyond the illustrations offered in the textbook. Talented educators recognize that the most effective framework for discovery may come from analysis of current events and case studies, not from recapping foundational theories and terminology alone.

Simply as a result of the publishing model that takes 18 to 24 months to issue a textbook, the content is outdated prior to the resource ever having been released. Consequently, this level of material timeliness and relevance is left for the faculty to supplement in the classroom. Carefully selected content promotes learning when faculty encourages students to challenge the veracity of ideas so the students experience this intellectual debate firsthand. In a learner-centered classroom, students do more than hear from the teacher about the work that biologists do; instead learners *do* the work themselves. The faculty creates this relationship of trust which, in turn, enables the student to feel safe in their pursuits of personal interpretation and direction, allowing curiosity of the adult learner to find firm roots to expand.

For some students, it is essential to dive in head first and to build meaning through the wonders of doing. This approach does not mean that they are in sophisticated labs pushing back the horizons of knowledge, but rather than having the teacher *tell* them how researchers collect observational data, the students *themselves* collect data. Rather than having the teacher offer them the outcome of a classic experiment, the adult learners are given the data and challenged to hypothesize about the results. Experiential learning supports the Knowles (1950, 1962, 1973, 1989) research where the adult learner must be given appropriate relevance to enhance their personal discovery as part of the educational experience.

Using content to promote the intellectual development requires active learning strategies. The goal is to challenge the ability of students to test their new-found skills, to work through as well as possibly struggle through the wonders of application, to discover the joys of creating a relationship with their environment. If the student develops the confidence to ask questions, they stretch themselves to isolate new conclusions that have merit beyond the classroom exchange itself.

Vantage Point #1: Administrators

As administrators are tasked with the selection and training of faculty for the student experience, the challenges are many regarding assessment of educator scholarship and andragogical technique versus student popularity. As administrators look to the profit motive to drive student enrollment or retention, there are many masters to serve. What becomes the priority and the central driving force? Is the classroom experience truly a transactional business exchange where the administration exists to serve the popularity and entertainment needs as demanded by the student as well as accreditation standards demanded by the Higher Learning Commission, an accepted guardian of intellectual rigor and discourse? As budgets continue to be paired down, where is the focus? Where are the priorities? What may be comprised in the pursuit of balance? Has the true mission of education been somehow lost in the process or intentionally disregarded? Has the profit motive drowned out intellectual fundamentals?

From a big picture perspective, administrators may find

value in training faculty in the use of effective andragogy in the classroom. This approach may enhance practice competencies to strengthen interpersonal interactions with learners and may forward the process of exploring new information and make it more engaging. Further, faculty may heighten the level of interest in the material, resulting in higher retention and knowledge transfer levels. Clearly, shifts in practice serve both the institution and the student by making content more meaningful. In a time of economic turmoil and dwindling retirement accounts, education can provide opportunity for continued intellectual and experiential development, serving the needs of many masters.

Vantage Point #2: Faculty

Post-secondary educators can elect to adopt an empowering personal teaching philosophy. Faculty can emulate the distinct advantages of critical and refractive thinking to change the world through education—"one student and one mind at a time" (Lentz, 2009b). The advantages of a learner-centered focus are that the faculty becomes immersed in creating the stage upon which the student actively participates. Instead of being continually led through lecture and highly structured content, the student directs their own learning. Faculty model, through demonstration and example, how to use critical and refractive thinking skills to view and interpret their world.

Probing questions such as "What does the data from a scientific experiment mean?" [and] "What lessons might an in-class interactive lesson offer?" help learners to draw their own connections, to illicit creative questioning, and to wonder. The faculty member then becomes an accountability coach to ensure that the student is on target and on task with completion of learning objectives. What different ideas might a student learn when the faculty functions as a guide and a tutor, perhaps coach? Do students know enough to demand such control in this way for their educational pursuits? "Christopher Jencks and his colleagues claimed that 'schools serve primarily as selection and certification agencies, whose job is to measure and label people, and only secondarily as socialization agencies, whose job is to change people' " (Arum & Roksa, 2011, p. 51). Is this more dynamic approach simply a natural evolution of education?

The lessons here are that if students will rise to meet faculty expectations, should faculty have the courage to stretch and raise the bar to teach for the sake of learning and knowledge acquisition? To do so requires a shift from being concerned with end-of-course surveys and the potential function of popularity.

Vantage Point #3: Students

Arum and Roksa (2011) suggested that "undergraduate education is fundamentally a social experience" (p. 59). A student they interviewed aptly summarized that "one's 'social life' shouldn't necessarily come at the expense of [one's] studies (or) the overall goal of graduation" (Arum & Roksa, 2011, p. 59). Is this what students intended when enrolling in post-secondary programs? Is academic success achieved through "controlling college by shaping schedules, taming professors, and limiting work load?" (Arum & Roksa, 2011, p. 59). When did a shift in expectations occur and should this path continue in this direction?

What do these signals mean? According to Psychologist William Damon, a growing number of adolescents lack purpose (as cited in Arum & Roksa, 2011). Students have been studying 4 hours or more less per week as a result of the social distraction element (Arum & Roksa, 2011). The learner looks at the opportunity of a return on investment (ROI) of their time. The focus thereby becomes a business transactional exchange or opportunity cost. Subsequently, the learner examines where he or she can receive the most return on their investment. Does the student feel more demand to play with Facebook than to study, as it is an entertaining diversion rather than a directed cognitive activity? As a result, students prone to this self-created intellectual poverty may seek a synopsis and read highlighted, bold sections of the material rather than pondering the historical discussion or focusing on the more salient—and potentially complex—elements of the chapter.

The paradigm shifts affects economics as well where "Today's students do not view debt exclusively as an investment, but also as a vehicle for consumption" (Arum & Roksa, 2011, p. 86). The learner as consumer or *consumer learner* offers a vastly different perspective than in times past and the viewpoint of prior learners. The question is whether this is an acceptable direction for education to continue to travel. Or, conversely, is it the role of post-secondary institutions to adapt to driving market conditions?

With the football games and the myriad of social clubs taken out of the online educational focus the outcomes do not change. What then is the purpose of the first tier of post-secondary education in the nontraditional undergraduate college or university? Is the goal to learn about oneself as well as the curriculum? Is there a way to serve both masters particularly as the costs of the college *social* experience continue to rise? Will parents continue to find this a fair exchange for their tuition dollars?

Those who come back to school as an older student or first embark upon a program as an adult learner, do not always have the advantage of being fully immersed and dedicated to their academic program. Learners must creatively address the added distractions of family demands, work demands, and, potentially, the need to care for their own aging parents. What are the preconditioned intellectual and experiential attributes students then need to succeed? Where does life balance enter the equation?

SUMMARY

The higher cost of degree attainment (both in terms of financial commitment and time) already significantly impacts student enrollment and retention. Less competitive post-secondary systems may potentially face obsolescence as a result. The market evolution has become lead, follow, or get out of the way.

While faculty give the adult learner *the opportunity,* the student must decide *their ability* to use the educational experience to greatest effect. The student/faculty relationship is intended as a joint partnership. The faculty is there to offer explanation however; an educator cannot help if they are not asked. The student's obligation is to recognize their needs that require clarity. A faculty can 'take a proverbial horse to water,' yet even though they cannot be made to drink, students can, potentially, be encouraged to feel the *thirst*.

CHAPTER 6

Technology as a Tool for Educational Transformation

THE INTRODUCTION OF THE WORLD WIDE WEB or *Internet*, as it was popularized in the early 1990s provided postsecondary administrators with a complex, yet promising, expansion opportunity. Rather than taxing physical plant resources to address the needs of a burgeoning student population, institutions could compensate for crowded classrooms and packed-to-capacity instructional sections by providing curriculum through an electronic platform. This innovative delivery mechanism brought the potential for efficiency, lean management of the system infrastructure, and a new capacity for reaching learners. Simultaneously, however, the rich potential of technology also generated never-before-encountered implications in the areas of structuring meaningful content, measuring curriculum effectiveness, and monitoring student integrity as there was no definitive way to confirm the identity of the individual on the other side of the screen in the *virtual classroom*.

Through both concurrent or synchronous delivery, and independent or asynchronous action, students experienced a new way to gain their education and pursue a course of study. This evolution continues to broaden in scope as the current online modality considers tools enhancements. Illustrations include mobile application (or mobile app) delivery tools, interactive live programs within the online delivery platform such as Blackboard, Angel, Moodle, and others. Universities are increasingly creating unique responses to include a main technical support for computers as well as a separate and distinct mobile app departments.

Technology is both the engine that drives the online learning platform (such as Blackboard or eCollege, on a macro level) and is delving deeper into the micro level from the integration or real time video enhancements to chat programs. Other innovations include synchronous components such as WIMBA Live Classroom or Instant Messaging (IM) platforms, which offer both text and video to chat (creating an interactive office hour component for learners and educators alike). This approach offers both the student and the faculty the ability to enhance or engage in a synchronous model with elements of real time synchronous technologies, radically changing the way online instruction is offered. Are these techniques simply part of the *edutainment* expectation and experience? Will faculty have to retool, retrain, and redesign andragogical strategies as a result? Do educators yet know what techniques within these new design structures provide for effective learning outcomes?

Educators must continually examine the question of how these new evolutions serve the andragogical need of students. Do they effectively support or potentially compromise the pursuit of intellectual discourse and learning outcomes? Is the learning enhanced by the integration of multi-faceted techno gadgets such as Skype, Talk Fusion, chat, and mobile app functions? Are these simply game components as part of the *edutainment* experience or proven andragogical methods?

In its contemporary form, distance education includes courses and programs formally designated as online, hybrid/blended online (combination of online and in-class instruction with reduced in-class seat time for students), and other approaches and programs. Technology enhanced education within the post-secondary environment has emerged as an area of immense reinterpretation and expansion. Commonly touted advantages include convenience/ease of access to educational content and degree acquisition, focused instructional guidance, and content that demands reflection.

According to the U.S. Department of Education, National Center for Education Statistics 2008 report, 66% of the 4,160 Title IV degree-granting postsecondary institutions in the nation offered college-level distance education courses in the 2006/2007 school year. The statistics break down to 97% of public 2-year institutions, 18% of private for-profit 2-year institutions, 89% of public 4-year institutions, 53% of private not-for-profit institutions, and 70% of private for-profit 4-year institutions (U.S. Department of Education, National Center for Education Statistics, 2008).

The U.S. Department of Education (2008) report also indicated that 65% of the institutions reported college-level credit-granting distance education courses, and 23% of an estimated 12.3 million enrollments (or individual course registrations) were in noncredit distance education courses. Conclusions drawn from the analysis show 77% of students were in online courses, 12% in hybrid/blended online courses, and 10% attributed to other forms of distance education courses (U.S. Department of Education, National Center for Education Statistics, 2008).

Rather than viewing distance learning as an area of concern

and great challenge, the post-secondary educator can embrace the idea that this methodology enhances access and opportunity. Several very specific advantages exist: online benefits provide the instructor with the ability to carefully craft a post. He or she can conduct additional research, and repeat this inquiry process until clarity and proper andragogy is found. Conversely, in the on ground classroom, the educator must be precise with their articulation the first time. He or she risks the potential for misinterpretation or flawed delivery of a complex message.

Another benefit of the electronic forum is the educator can more accurately evaluate the power of the written word. This process ensures that salient ideas are absorbed as the students demonstrate comprehension both within one answer, and as integrated throughout the course. Assessment through the weekly written assignments and discussion posts provides validation of what was understood, and what bears repeating. These are opportunities that are missed in the on ground familiar due to having to depend on memory recall week-to-week and throughout the continuity of one course, term, or semester. Distance learning curriculum is, by nature, highly experiential. Students gain vital lessons in virtual team skills, and how to work with people they cannot *see* and have never met—which cultivates an increasingly important business competency treasured in many industrial environments, particularly with the expansion of globalization. In this area, students judge work based on how the tasks are linguistically conveyed, missing elements of the traditional communication sender/receiver model that includes nonverbals. While it is possible to still use nonverbals to enhance the communication model, the techniques differ as might the approach. New adaptations from foundational skills are needed to gain proficiency in this area when one lacks face-to-face contact.

Technology as a Tool for Educational Transformation

Contributors to the emerging dialogue gain understanding of diversity as the virtual classroom provides participants with access to students of other ethnicities and cultures well beyond the demographic distribution that may be found in a local campus classroom. Perhaps most importantly, by modeling effective professional communication, strategic thinking, thoughtful analysis, and through emphasis on the transfer of concepts, terminology and discovery, educators underscore the importance of thoughtfulness and tolerance. Learners can illustrate the value of making a quality impression the first time and/or within solely electronic means. If one is applying for a job for example and networking online with colleagues/classmates is the only option, the asynchronous environment can enable the cultivation of valuable personal strengths in negotiation, compromise, and persuasion.

Effective collaboration and competent communication are not, however, a given in distance education. There is certain anonymity of teams, for example, which may lead learners to behave with disrespect or without a genuine commitment to deadlines. Accountabilities may be dropped and the caliber of work compromised. When addressing the large issue of quality control, there is yet another dimension that factors into the dilemma of proper use on the online modality. How are these differences taught and addressed? Will orientation classes now be needed to potentially reteach adjustments to communication and courtesy and manage within these new virtual classrooms? How will these skills be taught? While all educational environments should reflect courtesy toward faculty and peers, displaying an appropriate disposition and conversational tone appear to be larger issues in this forum.

Educators have increasingly reported verbal and interpersonal abuse from online learners who refuse requests for private dialogue with the professor. Students challenge the educator's authority in the learning process by creating disruption in the chat and discussion forums, and by logging posts to the full classroom rather than resolving his or her specific performance issues or grading challenge in a more professional, and acceptable manner. Under the guise of anonymity, students seem to be finding a new boldness or audacity that they would not dare to exhibit in a face-to-face environment. Privacy, and the ability to share personal information seems, too often to cross the line as well.

Rather than focusing on their individual accountabilities and rising to the benchmark level of performance, students may attempt to derail the online class, and garner learner community support through targeted challenges and unproductively channeled criticism. The potential for this form of disruption means the educator must be fluent in procedures, work hand-in-hand with administrates to reiterate policies, and thoroughly document the behavior.

A further consideration in the online learning environment emanates from the rich, continuing dialogue that may be cultivated. Expansive exploration of ideas means it is entirely possible students may ask charged questions that are political in nature or that question conventional thinking. To cultivate productive, guided inquiry, while limiting derailing contributions, institutional leadership must precisely—and routinely—examine policies regarding online techniques and decorum.

Students may erroneously conclude there is a level of informality present in online programs. Subsequently, learners may not model business suit etiquette, which is an essential requirement for productive interaction. This may be due, in part, to the comfort level learners feel in technologically assisted forums which "allow for a degree of freedom and autonomy for youth that is less apparent in a classroom setting. Youth respects one another's authority online and they are often more motivated to learn from peers than from adults" says Arum and Roksa (2011, p. 61).

The last and most significant concern regarding online learning to be addressed here is the question of rigor. Administrators, curriculum designers, and educators must effectively capitalize on the strengths of online and distance education, without neutralizing the effectiveness of the learning experience. Students must emerge from a course with a solid grasp of the content, and demonstrated proficiencies in the stated outcomes. Those learners, who do not meet the minimum expectations of the course, cannot be allowed to proceed toward completion. Intervention and appropriate guidance is required to ensure that each student appropriately fulfills the course requirements.

This chapter suggests some of the most pressing multifaceted concerns that surround online learning. It is clear that to be effective, this transformational mechanism for conveying educational programs requires continual assessment. An emphasis must be placed on upgrading technology and improving process to ensure that the very vulnerabilities of this delivery method which may compromise the authenticity and legitimacy of student work and performance to measurable outcomes are continually examined.

Vantage Point #1: Administrators Tool for Business Model

In the last 5 years, the delivery of online classes and complete educational programs has caused rapid enrollment growth (Moloney & Oakley, 2006). In addition to infrastructure challenges, this period has emerged as an area of immense reinterpretation and expansion for many U.S. post-secondary institutions. Commonly touted advantages include convenience and ease of access to educational content and degree acquisition, focused instructional guidance, and content that demands reflection.

Variance exists in administrators' and faculty perceptions of the online learning framework. Connolly, Jones, and Jones (2007) contend that while some institutions insist online education is crucial for long-term viability, other institutions consider online learning as a means to increase short-term enrollment (Allen & Seaman, 2007). Burge (2008) attributed some of the dissention in opinions to the disposition toward change found in institutional methodology. Allen and Seaman (2007) acknowledged the unparalled growth in this area, but also wonder if institutions will reach capacity limits due to a fluid market of new students and the high cost of expanding services. It is entirely possible that in the future, more students will desire technology facilitated instruction and administrators and faculty must address a potentially unwelcome paradigm shift from campus-based delivery to a distance education heavy platform.

Technology assisted education enables education enables the institution to remove traditional access barriers such as geographic positioning in a community, the timing of course delivery, or the over-crowding on campuses. Further, it is easier—and significantly more cost-effective—to add new sections in the online modality, as specialized faculty can be recruited from across the nation. When executed with precision, the online programs provide lucrative financial opportunities for institutions of higher learning and infuse the general budget with much-needed funds. Alignment with the corporate community was intended to produce students capable of meeting the needs of the business realm. Institutions of higher learning may wish to eagerly and proactively embrace this opportunity to boost profitability and to survive in the current economic climate.

Administrators are no longer just administrators within post-secondary education with the goals of educating only students of business for business. Administrators must embrace the adjustment from the vantage point of a traditional academic to one that includes for-profit business models for its own future viability.

The controversy that is emerging in this area, however, is whether to maintain or to lift pre-requisites. Does creating greater opportunity move the focus on a degreed curriculum then transition to an emphasis on a certification culture? If the shift serves students, why then should administration feel the need to apologize if the institution purposely engages in innovation pursuits (such as those modeled by for-profit educational institutions) to attract and retain students?

Vantage Point #2: Faculty

Within the on ground classroom, technology becomes a tool of enhancement to previous tenets of andragogy. The *consumer learner* is expecting more than the traditional lecture mode/method. Instead, the student desires entertainment. Is the online delivery classroom a viable tool that serves the andragogical needs of the educational model? Does this support a *USA Today* model of teaching—the teaching practice of highlighting content in sound bytes and brief captions? Does this compression model work as a valid method of post-secondary instruction? For example, how do you compress a 40-page chapter in a required text down to a one salient discussion question? Does the process of matching the material to the delivery method comprise the integrity of the ideas in some way?

While faculty may be enamored with the idea of providing greater access to students, some hold the opinion that educational quality may have been compromised or somehow thwarted by the administrative priority to purse profit through expanded delivery modalities. A key dilemma is whether the format provides a mechanism for dishonest conduct by students. For example, how does the educator authenticate the person/voice behind the screen or telephone? Is the registered learner actually taking the class and completing the required assessments or is someone masquerading to gain higher scores? Similarly, privacy concerns exist, and educators must take great care to uphold the Family Educational Rights and Privacy Act (FERPA). Subsequently, changes in student-educator communication are needed, and grades/generalized performance feedback must be provided through genuinely transparent, real-time grading systems.

Vantage Point #3: Students

By enhancing the portability of education, students may enjoy higher levels of degree completion. Additionally, because of the required mastery of technology, online education is both sensible and highly appropriate for the Twitter generation. The evolution and emergence of the online modality is expedient, convenient, and information is provided in a familiar framework. The performance challenges come in formulating content and developing ideas into fully formed, expressive paragraphs. Technical proficiency must be accompanied by effective use of logic and outlining. Grammatical competency also is required, as is excellence in citation practices. Because of the fast-paced delivery cycle, the student must have self-initiative and strictly adhere to deadlines and performance expectations. It is, unfortunately, easier to hide in the online modality.

Entertainment is another factor to consider as a result of greater societal culture with the expansion of Twitter and Facebook, not just as a social media, but expansion to the companies, and media outlets. It is clearly changing the expectations of what a student would like to see in the classroom. There is an expectation that because the medium of educational delivery is different the convenience and efficiency translate into easier classes with regard rigor and intellectual learning objectives and outcomes.

SUMMARY

This chapter suggests some of the most pressing multi-faceted concerns that surround online learning and distance education. A reasonable conclusion to draw is that to be effective, this transformational mechanism for conveying educational programs requires continual assessment. An emphasis must be placed on upgrading technology and improving processes to ensure that the very vulnerabilities of this delivery method which challenge authenticity and legitimacy of student work and performance to measurable outcomes are continually examined.

Initially at least, the primary concern in regards to online education surrounded the best process for rapid delivery of information and reliable technical system performance. Students required formatted content that was intuitive to follow and reliably available. This new modality of learning quickly created a curriculum specialization as it became critical to *package* progressive educational experiences, and to keep the class moving together toward course outcome achievement. Educators concurrently developed best practices for engaging students, and guiding them through course materials in a manner that reflected integration. The professorate discovered through trial, error and ingenious experimentation, mechanisms for transforming the post-secondary scholastic experience.

At first a supplement to the traditional on ground classroom, the online—or distance education—format became a way to provides formal exposure to units of study, and to mandate substantial student participation standards without the requirement of a physical, onsite presence. What began as distance education has evolved into the platform of the online modality. As the evolution of these unique delivery methods emerged, modality continued, and the notion of distance education encompassed video and audio capacity. Through both concurrent or synchronous delivery, and independent or asynchronous action, students experienced a new way to gain their education, and pursue a course of study. This transformation continues as the current online interpretations now consider access tools enhancements such as mobile application (or mobile app) delivery tools, interactive live programs within the platform such as Blackboard, Angel, Moodle and others. To further this expansion of service, universities are creating unique responses to include a main technical support for computers and even separate and distinct mobile app departments.

Educators must return once again to the question of how these new approaches serve the andragogical needs of students. Specifically, it is essential to consider how technologies enhance or detract from the pursuit of intellectual discourse and learning outcomes as well as that of the student overall experience.

CHAPTER 7

Measures of Success and Outcomes

MANY EDUCATIONAL THEORISTS, among them Brookfield (1987, 1991, 1992), have expressed concern that adult learners are inadequately prepared to function fully within a society based on democratic processes. Executives are likely to agree that a wider range of competencies that require competent assessment and decision-making that is essential in today's highly competitive industries. To ensure that students possess the abilities to contribute meaningful performance, new ways of evaluating the transfer of skills from the classroom to the real world are needed.

The adult teaching model upon which this theory of education (as a mechanism through which the individual gains attributes of benefit to society) is predicated appears to lack rigor. Further, the purposeful integration of practice and thought has generated a transformational shift from a teaching-centered to a learning-centered paradigm. In this emerging paradigm, Barr and Tagg (1995) see the primary purposes of colleges and universities as production learning, rather than providing instruction, and traditional teaching as only one of many means of learning (Angelo as cited in "Classroom Assessment Techniques," 2002, p. 4). The focus thereby becomes enabling the adult student to gain transferrable strategies that have value beyond the attainment of the college degree itself. To understand what is gained, and how the processes themselves may be enhanced, it is essential to cultivate a more refined understanding of how learning outcomes are determined, and how they are ultimately achieved.

The most simplistic definition of assessment is offered by Palloff and Pratt (2006). To be effective these authors suggested that the assessment must be "learner-centric, teacher-directed, mutually beneficial, formative, context-specific, ongoing, and firmly rooted in good practice" (p. 1). This definition supports a philosophy focused on the dynamics of the relationship of the adult learner and faculty, as well as the synergy of the students within their classroom. The adult learner needs to know *what* they are doing and *why*, and *how* each activity that is required aligns with the instructional approaches that are used in the course. "Assessments should be formative—meaning that they occur throughout the course and inform practice—and summative—meaning that they occur at the end of the course and assess cumulative learning from the course" (Palloff & Pratt, 2006, p. 1).

A student therefore begins the process of engaged learning by recognizing the need to understand the course and resultant learning, from their point of view (Smith, 2008). "The more meaningful the course, the more likely that they [the adult learner] will develop into empowered and lifelong learners" (Palloff & Pratt, 2006, p. 4).

The assessment and evaluation process is crucial to developing well-rounded and holistic adult learners who are skilled critical thinkers. To create dynamic individuals who literally function as *consumer learners* who process and apply ideas with integrity, curiosity and integrity "students and their teachers become partners in the classroom assessment process" (Stiggins & Chappuis, 2006, p. 11). The synergy of this process helps provide additional guidance with proven strategies to increase student learning and relevancy for a more effective outcome.

For many educators, this increased popularity within the online modality has necessitated a shift in pedagogical technique [or the newly adopted term andragogical (adult) technique] from a "teacher-centered, test-based, outcome-based approach to a more student-centered, process-based, or project-based approach" (Sanders as cited in Comeaux, 2005, p. 18). This shift in focus offers a more in-depth discovery of the process and outcomes of learning (Biggs, 1996). In addition, this philosophical view offers the educator an opportunity to encourage more authentic learning outcomes that are more closely connected with the needs of the student on a more personal level. This integration then forces the reevaluation of the assignment rubric and specific feedback elements with regard to the student as part of this adjusted process.

By taking a long-term approach to learning—what has the student learned from a summative standpoint—the reflection is within a broader context, moving away from a week-by-week formative approach, to a scope that includes deeper dialogues on the material for a more purposeful exchange with the student. Therefore, two levels of inquiry are needed: a micro level of content mastery—does the student begin with a basic understanding of the materials and the macro level of a larger understanding of application within *context* of the overall scope of the course. The performance assessment at the micro level offering the most effective outcome would then be the weekly quizzes, self-directed content mastery exercises, and other exercises where the student is responsible for the acquisition of *term specific* knowledge.

Once this foundational thinking is mastered, the faculty can truly be a facilitator—to offer further guidance to the student that focuses on integration and application. A true synthesis of the materials is then gained. Therefore the focus of the rubric for end-of-course summative project assignments needs to be assessed less on content. The concentration must move to application and conceptual adaptation that asks the student to apply their knowledge, not simply demonstrate their understanding of the building blocks *of* that knowledge. "Accordingly, these teaching methods require a [more] dynamic, continuous, and performance-based assessment system that emphasize[s] progress in learning and in becoming increasingly sophisticated learners and knowers (Huba & Freed, 2000)" (as cited in Comeaux, 2005, p. 19).

Perhaps the priority should shift to the idea of *progressive* student feedback and assessment. Here is where educators hold diverse views. Some, such as Mollem (2005) suggested there is a movement away from individual self-assessment. Others contend that a self-directed emphasis of the student being responsible for content mastery can be challenging for students with a *less than the ideal* prerequisite knowledge base. These students depend more heavily on the educator to serve as guide and mentor, which requires a greater investment of time on the part of the faculty. This is where an even larger focus must be highlighted. The burden is on the institution as well as the overall connection of the program design course-to-course to create perspective. Collectively, this illustrates how newly acquired knowledge has pertinence in the learner's business setting.

Faculty must become more responsible beyond their role in

the current class functioning instead as a link in a continual chain that serves student development and enhancement. Students must be forced to retain their content mastery knowledge as they progress through their academic program for each faculty member to have the capacity to build upon this understanding. In doing so, the post-secondary educator takes the student to the next level—at the macro plane of learning where "anchoring all learning activities to a larger project or problem and assessing students' learning outcomes by directly observing their performance in a real-world project" (Mollem as cited in Comeaux, 2005, p. 21) transpires. Subsequently, the faculty's application of feedback through the use of the grading rubric is driven by student learning.

There is considerable evidence showing that assessment motivates and directs learners. More than anything else, the choice of tools applied by a given institution expresses to students what educators consider to be important. Students will learn what they are directly guided to learn through the assessments ("Assessment Primer," 2010, para. 2). Therefore, the evaluative elements of what is included within the grading rubric become crucial to the student's success. This rubric is no longer a linear checklist-based performance assessment of whether the student mastered the materials or failed to demonstrate understanding. This approach can potentially strengthen the learner's ability to understand this new level of performance assessment. The carefully constructed grading rubric then becomes a tool for *the student's own personal learning* as well as the faculty member's *confirmation* of learning. The student becomes an integral component and advocate for their own academic outcomes, where the rubric is merely a tool in their hands as well as that of their faculty.

By training the student to use previous feedback from the

instructor, as well as including the grading rubric as part of their editing process, there may need to be some investment of time beyond the content scope of the faculty. Often students are given access to tools but lack the conceptual understanding of how to efficiently integrate and use them effectively as part of a student-centric focus.

Therefore a reasonable argument can be made that traditional use of the grading rubric offers a very limited measure of student learning—and more important—authentic meaning for the overall experience for the adult student, particularly in the online and distance education environment. By changing the boundaries of technology, more emphasis is placed on the shoulders of the learner. This news is particularly positive and effective with the increased popularity and the convenience of the online modality, as more of the adult learner population is being attracted to this method. As a result, faculty need to adjust both the conceptual understanding of the contemporary learner and their reasons to pursue higher education. Additionally, the assessment process of the grading rubric and feedback loop must then be addressed in the larger context of the student experience (Brookfield, 1987).

Vantage Point #1: Administrators

The mark of an institution's success is commonly measured through matriculation rates. When business publications such as *U.S. News and World Report*, for example, rank colleges and universities, primary criteria is the total number of degrees conferred. Another consideration is how closely the institution adheres to accreditation policy. A third pertinent view is whether programs qualify for specialized certification through industry validation of educational programming, where ultimately, the graduation rates and other achievements are aligned with the efficiency of the system.

In a time when institutions are externally evaluated based on their student's assumption of debt upon graduation, the traditional measures are an incomplete form of assessment. Another key performance indicator is the subsequent placement of graduates within industry, which may be viewed as the ultimate assessment of learning attainment.

Vantage Point #2: Faculty

The movement toward a temporary workforce of adjunct faculty versus full-time, tenured educators has altered the business model of a system that has traditionally honored longevity. Now, the high level of reliance on part-time practitioners adjusts the institution's financial hierarchy while displacing the emphasis on curriculum consistency.

While the grading rubric remains a necessary element to the assessment of the final course project, it must offer a deeper and more meaningful dialogue with the student with a broader and longer-term focus. "Critical thinking is a capacity recognized as important not just by educators, helping professionals, academic psychologists, and philosophers, but by most adults themselves" (Brookfield, 1987, pp. 48–49). Consequently, the circle is complete with more diverse assessments of authentic student experiences to enable effective learning outcomes.

Vantage Point #3: Students

A prevailing view appears to be 'pay your fee, get your D' as students increasingly interpret the educational process as a business transaction. While some do pursue a degree for the true love of learning and intellectual curiosity, many *consumer learners* are looking at post-secondary experiences as a means to an end. They enroll in a program with a sense of purpose, and an expectation of a financial return on their investment (ROI). An emerging point of controversy is that some students have even challenged the relevancy of a degree in a downturn economy if their new credentials fail to help them realize a job.

The intention of a degree is to provide perspective, literacy with the functional terms, concepts and theories, and enhanced ability to transfer this new knowledge. This does not ensure that the acquisition of a degree alone improves one's marketability (employment potential), but that is a real-world driver for many learners. Increasingly, graduates are questioning the level of debt incurred for their programs and wondering if the value proposition will be fulfilled.

In an employer-choice market, recruiters seek the best and most qualified candidates. In some cases, the individual who appears qualified on paper lacks a sound experiential base. Conversely, the individual with a wide scope of experience lacks the refined critical thinking skills and analysis abilities extended by the college graduate. The problem of which applicant is most suitable intensifies as the learner presents graduate and doctorate preparation. The dilemma thus faced by the employer is which profile will ultimately provide the best match to the organization's requirements.

SUMMARY

As a pay-for-performance or pay-per-student-enrolled model becomes predominant, compensation for most educators has been moved from a minimum of classes to a limit which benefits the institution above the instructor. This benefit model extends

Measures of Success and Outcomes

advantages to the administrators, yet compromises the earning potential of faculty.

Educators are assessed on multiple levels in this emerging paradigm. One measure is popularity with students based on their direct involvement in the rating of instructors, with the purpose being an inquiry into the learner's level of satisfaction. Other measures include student retention, which is increasingly and ubiquitously defined as student success rates. A concern that may become subordinate in the big picture is the educator's legitimate ability to fulfill the requirements of the course objectives based on accreditation standards.

More than ever before, the student has a choice of voting with their educational dollars. Learners can seek institutions that address both their program requirements and their preferred learning style. Further, they can seek a comfortable fit in terms of program delivery format and applicable timing, and ultimately, their ideal advantages gained from their level of financial investment.

CHAPTER 8

The Path of Least Resistance

TO BE ACTIVELY ENGAGED *CONSUMER LEARNERS,* students must first recognize the significance of their disposition toward the educational process. It is critical to distinguish the difference between *effort* and *outcome.* Corporations do not compensate employees for simply showing up each day, but for substantial performance. If the condition of expectation met by achievement is adopted, a new performance model emerges. Recognition is then placed on integrity efforts toward productive—even potentially transformational—outcomes. This is, in essence, a *Rocking Chair Strategy.* While students are busy *rocking away* in their rocking chair, does the chair move forward in any way? Typically, the answer is no as students instead, simply appear busy with *efforts,* not the accomplishment of *outcomes.*

Conversely, the academic community must encourage the student to develop a learning goal orientation. Grounded in research conducted by Dweck (1986), this view was expanded by VanderWalle, Cron, and Slocum (2001). These authors stated that focus must be placed on "developing one's competence by acquiring new skills, mastering new situations, and learning from experience" (p. 100).

Post-secondary educators cannot allow learners to become focused on movement—shuffling papers from point A to point B—as essential results such as critical thinking growth are not achieved. The objective must become building learners who are accomplished, fully engaged, analytical individuals who apply what is gained in the educational journey to their professional and personal lives.

To realize this shift, it is essential for the professoriate to acknowledge how easily students can become consumed by the physical commitment to education. Learners may show up for class, but are they intellectually present? Are they fully invested in the academic activities of the course? Do they proactively seek out transfer opportunities that improve their ability to contribute to industry and to foster advanced problem assessment skills?

Adding complexity to this challenge is the realization that it is often easy for the adult learner to confuse their efforts with their self-identity. An academic grade may be seen as a reward for effort, rather than the result of achievement against an objective milestone. The philosophical divide that arises here between the educator and the learner is that the former is required to assess and to judge the contribution, and the later must strive to achieve a ranking—a grade—through specific *outcomes*. It is essential for the performer to actually meet grading criteria as established by a respective collegiate program. A clear message must be consistently conveyed to today's *consumer learner:* a grade of A is earned, not awarded for merely showing up. The *consumer learner* recognizes the potential of an outcome-based strategy. The concentration moves to visualizing the ultimate accomplishment (normally the acquisition of a degree) and then works backwards to ensure appropriate levels of learning occur. The individual subsequently emerges through the experience as more competent and self-aware.

Vantage Point #1: Administrators

Walter, Knudsvig, and Smith (2003) suggested students should seek relevance in their studies to enhance comprehension. "Strong critical thinkers are people who can take what information is before them and assimilate it into what they already know" (p. 48). Further, they have the capacity to "accommodate information that is new or in conflict with what they know or believe" (Walter et al., 2003, p. 48). Although these learners do not hesitate to formulate answers, they are "always ready to adjust their answers and perspectives based on new and valid information" (Walter et al., 2003, p. 48).

Cognitive learners look for associations, and draw parallels. By isolating the similarity of ideas, educators can ideally initiate a spark of curiosity to help the student to look beyond surface meanings and for substantial conclusions (Silver, 2011, website). Institutional leadership must, therefore, place greater emphasis on new forms of learner assessment. The concentration must zero-in on the most relevant measures for determining where transferrable knowledge has indeed been gained through the educational process.

Vantage Point #2: Faculty

The traditional post-secondary model relied on rigorous forms of learning assessment such as formal examinations, and written essays to judge content competency. When the most legitimate test of what is gained in the classroom rests on the *take-aways*, it is critical to evaluate student achievement based on what they can bring to industry.

Adult-oriented educators can encourage learners to surprise themselves by becoming directly engaged in their process of knowledge acquisition and transfer. They can be encouraged to recognize the value of critical thinking skills and, specifically, refractive thinking which takes them beyond assumptions and into innovative reflection without boundaries. The challenge becomes applying relevant methods to assess outcomes, and to validate—or even challenge—whether learning has transpired.

Vantage Point #3: Students

There seems to be a shift in focus among adult learners. Instead of the pursuit of excellence, students seem to be settling for the acceptance of mediocrity. What is the least effort that can be extended for the maximum reward? The primary goal is how to leverage the time, the money and the effort invested in the pursuit of the degree.

The adult learner is driven by efficiencies. He or she is sandwiched between the multiple demands of employment, family, and school. The overarching influence of a troubled economy places more pertinence on the need to diversify their skill set and to remain competitive in an increasingly global marketplace. Every investment, the largest of which may be the educational burden, must perform effectively. The student must be able to visualize a tangible value emerging from the pursuit of a degree. At the end, in addition to securing a diploma, the desire is a larger payoff—potentially being viewed as eligible for advancement and more stable, and long-term, employment.

SUMMARY

For the majority of current day degree holders who came through the traditional post-secondary experience, program completion symbolized the culmination of industrious effort. Conversely, the *consumer learner* interprets the experience from the perspective of an opportunity-cost advantage. The investment in the degree must realize a concrete result. Specifically, graduates seek some sense of promise in the workplace. They want the external recognition that a degree has merit in the eyes of current and future employers. If the investment/benefit relationship is achieved, and the burden of proof is met, the educational process has been a worthwhile endeavor.

This chapter examined the divergent philosophies shaping the administration, faculty and student points of view. Although each perspective has merit, there is a common recognition that that the perspective of the business environment in which the learner is employed is a pre-eminent influence. Is the primary factor in the emerging landscape of the institutions of higher education and learning driven by industry or is it now driven by the *consumer learner*?

CHAPTER 9

Classroom Culture

WHEN ADDRESSING THE IDEA OF CULTURE or climate, the individual is typically referencing the atmosphere and traditions of a particular industry or organization. If this conclusion is accepted, the potential inability of the faculty to achieve an effective setting might also suggest failure within the academic classroom. This interpretation of culture within the postsecondary setting offers intriguing ideas to consider regarding the three frames of reference applied in this work: administration, faculty, and students.

Leadership is modeled by the faculty when a class begins. The intention is to create a dynamic synergy that enhances student experience. Both learners and educators can often predict by the end of the first hour of class what kind of term it is going to be, and how potentially satisfied they will be with the overall experience. Another factor that shapes the instructional setting is found in the small signals which indicate early on what caliber of interpersonal relationships may be cultivated or challenged.

Culture offers a secondary, and ultimately unique and vital, point of departure for this chapter as there is both the culture within the classroom environment, and the disposition that the adult learner brings to the educational experience. The contemporary faculty member must adopt a *whole learner* perspective. This philosophy embraces the notion that the adult student is at once the employee, the parent, and the eager learner—all vantage points which are simultaneously juxtaposed against the constraints of time poverty.

Emerging technologies also shape the on ground classroom experience. The preponderance of techno gadgets from computers to tablets to cell phones—all offer tantalizing distractions which challenge the faculty member and require him or her to remain constantly vigilant to retain the student's attention. Some individuals have become so brazen that they will blatantly indulge in intentional multi-tasking texting. They may boldly express self-will through distracting behaviors, as they are more preoccupied with their life outside of the classroom than with their learning opportunities. The lack of courtesy on display from many adult students demonstrates that there is no subtle interest in hiding their behavior; they use their technology as an entitlement. Learners seem to find this conduct tolerable in other students, and not a violation of good etiquette or rudeness.

The consumptive obsession with these electronic gadgets furthers this unique culture of the *consumer learner*, extending the student-centric focus of the activities in the classroom as controlled by the individual. If bored, he or she purposefully tunes out the educator, viewing their disinterest as permission to find another outlet (such as Twitter or Facebook) to connect to content they enjoy. Rather than considering this choice even remotely questionable, exercising this option has become a socially acceptable practice—at least in the minds of the Gen Y student.

This raises the ethical concern of why there appears to be a politically acceptable nature to the inappropriate use of technology within the classroom. How can even the best prepared educator compete with the control the adult maintains, and their purposeful choice of self-diversion? Those who are digital immigrants (individuals who, for the most part, did not grow up with these devices, but have adapted to them) show more of a tolerance and mature knowledge of the appropriate time and place to rely on technology, and when to defer to professionalism. The serious adult learner more easily recognizes the efforts of an educator who is there to benefit the student, not function as a diversion.

However, it is also relevant to consider the convergence of these gadgets as learning tools in the classroom. When students are using their computers, tablets or cell phone as research tools to forward discussion, learning is advanced suggesting a sound, effective and real-time andragogical technique. If the results are constructive, should the faculty actually embrace and reward such behavior?

Vantage Point #1: Administrators

Technology has been welcomed into the classroom as it improves efficiency, profit-motive and marketing avenues to reach students. Further, it has a valuable role as a demonstration of current teaching enhancements. Students see the contemporary nature of the educational delivery model, while institutional leaderships see the attractiveness of this positioning in higher levels of student recruitment, enrollment, and retention.

Vantage Point #2: Faculty

Life does not stop for school, and a respite is not possible in demanding programs with concentrated delivery schedules. What level of attentiveness and participation is warranted from the student, versus desired by the practitioner? If students are present, and do not challenge the classroom culture with their use of personal technology, why should the educator object?
Adults can manage their own priorities without compromising comprehension. Further, they can independently determine what they need—and desire—to know. It is, therefore, the educator's obligation to make the content relevant and accessible.

Vantage Point #3: Students

Students function in a highly complex business settings that demand proficiency at multi-tasking. At the end of a long day, it is difficult to adjust this inclination when the educational process begins.

The myopic focus remains the *what's-in-it-for-me* dimension. Learners want to know if they do x, what y will look like, and be convinced of how instructional activities translate into value in the workplace. Technology is not a tool it is a necessity, and the student retains the privilege of using their time in the classroom in a way that satisfies their own expectations.

SUMMARY

Students frequently believe they are in a position to judge the merits of a quality educational experience. Administrators may support this view as they endorse the notion that satisfied learners emerge from the system as graduates. Faculty teeter on the balance beam between the two interpretations. As the direct purveyor of the service and the knowledge, the educator is accountable for the curriculum outcomes, and for the management of the classroom culture. If students eagerly participate in the relationship and model respect and curiosity toward colleagues and faculty, it is easier for measurement of progress to occur. If, however, learners are distracted and unfocused, the ability to assess what has been gained and understood is compromised.

So how is educational success ultimately accomplished in a responsive setting where learners sometimes have limited interest in the content? Is it possible for the academic to engage interest and to achieve involvement when students retain the capacity for choice?

CONCLUSION

Transitioning Toward a Mutually Beneficial Interpretation of Learning Consumption

Arguably, the most effective adult teaching model has experienced a powerful transformation in recent years. The emphasis has moved from being *teacher*-centric to a *learner*-centric focus (Barr & Tagg as cited in "Classroom Assessment Techniques," 2002). Knowles, Holton, and Swanson (2005) referred to this change as moving from the pedagogy technique for children (initially applied to adults) to the self-directed andragogy technique. This method dovetails nicely to support Wlodkowski's (1998) four-point motivational framework, particularly his concentration on relevancy and meaning. The adult learner wants to both discover *why*, and through his or her independent thought processes and self-directed learning, reaches conclusions that have personal meaning. Educators must, therefore, help adult learners to take responsibility for their educational endeavors and to look beyond prior student experiences (Knowles, 1990). The overarching intention should be for the student to "experience a need to learn it in order to cope more satisfyingly with real-life tasks or problems" (p. 40).

As addressed throughout this text, it is crucial for contemporary adult learners to acquire skills which demonstrate competency. The measure of success occurs at the completion of both the short-term process of course instruction, and through the larger goal of degree completion. The *consumer learner* strategically recognizes that it is essential to identify and then cultivate additional tools (such as theoretical understanding, relevant terminology, problem assessment and identification of alternative strategies), and the means of evaluating key results. This process of discovery adds to their repertoire of knowledge and capabilities within the larger business landscape. The educator's highly participatory role of guiding this acquisition is an element of effective course instruction (Knowles, Holton, & Swanson, 2005).

The post-secondary educator intentionally builds up, and expands, the elements of Socratic Questioning and self-directed skill acquisition. He or she encourages the student to build upon the initial desire of the learner for knowledge and to continually demonstrate the pertinence of ideas. By challenging the individual to think refractively, to move beyond conventional wisdom, to learn to challenge *what* they see, and most importantly to explain *why*, faculty help learners to recognize *what is already there*. This process expands the student's self-concept beyond their initial comfort zone and limitations, moving them toward active involvement in their educational experience and actual consumption of learning opportunities. Additionally, the process gives credence to adult teaching strategies where the goal is "an active process of translating new knowledge, insights, skills, and values into one's conduct" (Robinson, 1994, p. 3). As a result, this approach directly correlates to the outcome of adult learner behavior from theory to practice, to complete and to contribute balance to this adult learning cycle.

According to Brubacher and Rudy (2004), higher education in the United States is rooted within the humble beginnings of Yale and Harvard and the philosophies of human development that were maintained for nearly 200 years. It is only within contemporary generations that this provincial model of the intellectual elite has undergone radical shifts moving from a faculty-centric and scholarly stature to one of education being with reach of the masses. From the once hallowed halls of academia, to the impersonal boundaries of the cell phone—there has been quite a resounding transformation in perspective, focus, and outcomes.

Students are now the drivers of education, in charge of both their learning outcomes and potentially future business demands as they shift their education from one that began with learning the classics of Latin and philosophy, to the practicality of action research and faculty coaching as a legitimate process of learning. Only in time will history prove the adult learner to be right in their quest and approach. Perhaps this may be a calculated risk on the part of the adult learner? Will this direction and approach that challenges the conventional wisdom regarding adult learning ingrained within the nation's founding institutions hold the answer? While the exact future of the postsecondary model cannot be predicted its continued evolution is fascinating to consider.

The classics and philosophical dialogues of Socrates and Plato, and the literature masters of Chaucer and Thoreau, has given way to highly practical constructs. Perhaps Einstein was right when he stated, "No problem can be solved from the same consciousness that created it" (as cited in Stober & Grant, 2004, p. 113). The adult learner now faces a transactional business approach with truly measurable outcomes, instead of theoretical constructs. The concentration is on relatable concepts and immediately applicable discoveries that can be transferred into professional environments, rather than intellectual conclusions enjoyed merely for the joy of learning. In light of these changes, how will the success of knowledge acquisition be measured? Long gone are philosophical and intellectual discourse in favor of the practical *what have you done for me lately* approach. Students now evaluate curriculum, programs, and faculty from the position of utility; information must provide function and to serve an end purpose beyond content mastery. When considering this idea of measuring business outcomes in relation to educational pursuits, one must be objective and contemporary in the range of considerations addressed. Further, the review must encompass both success and failure. If a disparity of views were to exist, for example, what wins out—the foundational ideas or the highlights? Is content sacrificed for ease of transfer?

The last component of this notion of *consuming learning* is found in the discovery of pertinence gained from the process of persevering through challenge. Many adult learners cannot conceptualize that to have *success,* one must also have *failure.* The goal of tomorrow's collegiate faculty should be to convey the opportunity for experimentation within the safety net of the classroom—be it on ground or online. Students must be guided toward the acceptance of calculated risk as a mechanism for discovery and conclusion. Consumers of knowledge recognize that the ability to experience, cultivate, and strategically integrate the lessons of failure into the adult learning model brings perspective. Further, it fosters the recognition that business requires fluidity in thinking, and innovation is essential for commercial prosperity.

Conclusion

Post-secondary administrators and faculty must remember that an adult learner is an adult first. While the *consumer learner* can be gently and enthusiastically led, they need to have the motivation to accept the guidance and the commitment to perform in service of their ideals. Students must be well grounded in practical outcomes that can be measured in terms of dollars and cents, and directly translated into a return on investment (ROI). Very specifically, the objective is to lay a pathway for achieving a potentially higher paycheck.

EXPANDING EXPECTATIONS

Traditional teaching and university program structures are becoming obsolete—whether the progression is welcomed or challenged. Further, in addition to this shift, there is ample disagreement about the various levels of responsibility managed by those three parties in the educational triad: administrators, faculty and students. A secondary question is, if there are (arguably) discrepancies in the quality and satisfaction level experiences by those in the educational process who is accountable? Is institutional leadership responsible for program satisfaction, much like products are evaluated based on a combination of tangible and intangible factors/qualities? Is student failure a reflection on the instructor? Or conversely, is the student the main influence in their ability to thrive and achieve degree attainment, or their inability to meet the performance standards established in a given course?

Many in the profession of higher education may be quick to place the lion's share of the burden for competency squarely on the shoulders of the learner. There is merit in this view as the instructor cannot compel a student to listen attentively, to accurately comprehend the instructions for a given assignment, to make them complete the work by deadline, or to do so at a level of competency. The individual must be committed to their own successful performance in the class, strive to be organized, and focus on continual improvement.

Subsequently, learners can challenge what is sometimes seen as non-supportive, even arbitrary, systems of procedural actions such as tighter withdrawal and incomplete policies which may lead to lower GPA averages. Post-secondary educators could potentially see themselves as caught in a no-win scenario, sandwiched between the institutional mandates and the learners' preoccupation with excellent grades. This is another point of divergence in perceptions that is worth continued examination.

There is a new urgency being felt by the three partners as, increasingly, college degrees are viewed by industry as a screening device for a job. The academic setting serves essentially as an extension of the work performed in the business setting and expertise can often translate into the desired level of compensation. The pressures felt by all incorporated in the post-secondary environment are acute. While the traditional educational experience was highly social, today's learners must quickly—and hopefully proficiently—cultivate relevant knowledge gained through meaningful learning processes. Learners must be equipped to thrive in a world in which the specialist—rather than the generalist—has increased influence. In light of these environmental conditions, the post-secondary institution may continual its transformation, evolving from a bureaucratic model into a fluid structure that emulates the adaptability of industry.

The standards of education should transcend the actual delivery methods which are used to extend the product of discovery, and the encouragement of analytical conclusions. The strategic intention must center on becoming an interactive,

Conclusion

symbiotic system where student and educator are jointly committed to academic excellence. The educator cannot *drag* the student to the knowledge, he or she must willingly engage in the process.

In many ways, rather than disputing the emerging view of students as consumers, this text makes the case for learning as a transaction. Students do pay for their education with time, energy, and intellectual currency. There is a substantial financial and psychological investment in the acquisition of a degree. While grades must be earned through achievement, educators and administrators carry the accountability of providing curriculum elements and degree programs that offer the ability to gain competitive strengths that can be directly transferred into the increasingly crowded and complex global marketplace.

Where does the dialogue initiated in this work go from here? Clearly, adopting an understanding of the encompassing interpretation of the *consumer learner* means that all those engaged in the delivery and pursuit of higher education—administrators, faculty, and students—must strive to expand their vantage points. No one perspective is entirely reflective of the encompassing metamorphosis underway in the American post-secondary education model. Each constituency has pertinent reflections to share that warrant continued examination. To gain the most from this process of comparison, all of the partners involved in the creation and application of the learning transaction would be wise to work collaboratively. Together, the student customer mentality can be transitioned into a more positively directed *consumer learning* mentality. This approach places appropriate—and consistent—emphasis on active engagement and consumption of formal knowledge and transferrable experience as a progressive framework for life-long development.

QUESTIONS TO PONDER

Anheier (2005) contends that higher education is the second most economically significant field of nonprofit organizations in the United States. As demonstrated by the number of for-profit post-secondary institutions currently flourishing in the North American market, the industry's strength in the private sector cannot be challenged. For growth to continue, and learners to be best served, however, administrators must question what the future *looks like*, and innovate a path for successful growth and transition. Gamble (2010) suggested that when developing strategies it is essential to look at where the enterprise is currently, where leadership wants it to go, and how they are going to get there. While deceptively simple, these three questions constitute the business equivalent of critical thinking. If administration contemplates and reaches a decision about which direction to pursue, principle-based choices can be made that reflect institutional priorities and enable the realization of long-term viability, growth, and even reliable revenue generation. A critical element warranting discussion is the high cost of education. Van der Werf (2009) underscores that "More and more students are looking for lower-cost alternatives to attending college." Adult learners, in particular, have more life and perspective to incorporate in their educational activities and are savvier about comparing and contrasting post-secondary models and selecting institutions which meet their program and financial requirements. Van der Werf (2009) underscores that "More and more students are looking for lower-cost alternatives to attending college" (p. x). While community colleges and for-profit institutions may be highly successful at providing services to the underserved and non-traditional students, rapid enrollment growth will heighten the need for strategic change.

Conclusion

Does the method through which education is delivered matter? Is content king, and therefore is curriculum the core of a competitive educational product? Or is delivery its own independent entity?

The goal in this book was to initiate an emerging dialogue by contemplating these interesting dilemmas that technology and adaptive curriculum models now pose. Is an online component a standalone segment to the educational model, or simply an enhancement and a product differentiation to supplement existing models? Ultimately, which master is the priority? Initially, the notion of distance education was to look at ways to reach and serve the developmental aspirations of entities that were being underserved in the marketplace. Now technology is yet another tool in this innovative evolution of the educational process as a medium for an intellectual exchange of ideas.

The ambition here is not to evaluate or pass judgment, but to acknowledge the use of educational practitioner wisdom, collaboration, and integration of technology in an effective system that best serves the needs of the adult learner. How effectively the foundational objectives are met by the current state of the post-secondary education remains up to interpretation.

EPILOGUE

Stories From the Trenches, Contemporary Educational Challenges and Practices

AS WE BEGAN THIS JOURNEY, the desire was to open a dialogue with fellow colleagues, administrators, and students regarding the shift in the educational paradigm. A rich discourse in navigating these turbulent and fast moving waters of change has been initiated. Through a focus on the emergence of the consumer learners as an evolutionary step in the educational process, the intent is to offer meaningful examples and expressions of the lived student and practitioner experiences upon which this writing is based. We look forward to hearing your stories as well. Be certain to share your unique reflections and we will continue to move this exploration forward on our blog: http://www.consumerlearner.com. Additionally, look for our next work entitled: *Epilogue: Stories From the Trenches, Contemporary Educational Challenges and Practices*, coming in 2013 from Pensiero Press. Below please a preview of the content focus presented in that work which bridges from the content offered here in *The Consumer Learner: Emerging Expectations of a Customer Service Mentality in Post-Secondary Education.*

Example: Professor as Customer Service Agent

One pertinent example of the new context of post-secondary learning involves John. This individual was a 22-year-old online learner who could not seem to organize himself to meet deadlines. Mid way through the course, the student provided commentary to the instructor regarding how his busy work schedule did not afford him the opportunity to focus on his studies. While he seemed to take full accountability for his actions, the student nonetheless asked for an incomplete. When the educator informed the student he did not meet the criteria for an incomplete, the student rather sarcastically quipped that this decision "was not the customer service" he had expected. The faculty responded that the student did not feel his expectations were met only because he did not receive the answer he wanted. In his mind, the time spent together in the student-teacher exchange was merely a *transactional experience.* When the contract of the syllabus was knowingly broken on the individual's end, he still saw himself as the person buying the educational opportunity. He then expressed displeasure from the only vantage point he felt had credibility: "I paid for you to agree to my request. Failing to give me my preference is a failure in rendering customer service." The educator considered this reaction and wondered "When did I cease to be a professor, and became a customer service agent instead?"

Example: Student Confuses Showing Up with Accomplishment

Elaine, a graduate student, was clearly inattentive to assignment deadlines and accountabilities and earned a failing grade in the class. Upon receipt of her F, she disputed this grade saying "But I showed up. I should at least be given a C." She equated her sense of entitlement with attendance. She was of the Soccer Trophy Sect where she expected at least a C—for merely being physically present—even if she was not highly participatory and did not submit course work. This student confused attendance with accomplishment. In her mind, her physical presence was enough to earn her a passing grade. She completely missed the point of a *pay for performance model* in which points were acquired through successful completion of assignments, and discussion question responses that contributed to an emerging, and meaningful, dialogue. The student somehow lost focus that the measure of success was based on achieving specific outcomes. Achievement required an understanding of the expectations and recognition that this process was more involved than the act of merely occupying a desk in the classroom.

Example: All That Matters Is the Calculation

Consumer-oriented behavior is found in adult learners at all levels—a point made clear by one recent doctorate student, Grade-Conscious Gayle. After progressing slowly toward each assignment deadline and failing to incorporate technical and grammatical redirection from the educator, this individual still felt empowered enough to view a final grade as a negotiation. She reviewed the accumulated points with great care, quickly dispensing with the professor's targeted comments regarding continual improvement of the general writing and citation practices, and determined the range she found appropriate. As Gayle submitted the final milestone paper, she shared this note: "I realize I have been late, and my papers have been disappointments. Still, my GPA is vitally important. I ask that you give me at least a 92 percent on this paper so I will keep an A– in the class."

By articulating her preferences in this manner, Gayle was conveying two key points: 1) She understood that she failed to perform adequately, and 2) she wanted the bar lowered as, ultimately all that mattered was the grade on the transcript. No attention was paid to the issue of continuing errors in the work, and the failure to strive to be impressive and consistent in quality. The focus was on whether the educator would be *"appropriately"* accommodating.

Example: I'm Anonymous Behind the Screen

A highly confident undergraduate student—Bold Brad—registered for an online class. He expressed eagerness to participate in this interactive forum and immediately proved to be a lively addition to the discussion board. Unfortunately, however, the student also began to project a rather critical nature which he channeled most frequently toward female members of the class. At first, the comments were mild but demonstrated disagreement. Then, however, as learners failed to engage in a follow-up conversation, it became clear that Brad wanted to propel them into action. He began to challenge the strength of his peers' commentary. Statements became: "That conclusion was completely wrong" instead of "I saw it differently, how did you reach that decision?" Next, when students began tuning him out, Brad started to question the integrity of the discussion questions. Without a hint of hesitancy he posted that the content was incorrect and the inquiry without merit. He suggested the educator was in error to word the question in such a manner. To justify his comments Brad said he was relying on the textbook, but perhaps others (including the professor) were "reading it wrong and didn't get the idea."

Brad was a clever and otherwise engaged and solid student. The disposition problem that emerged was his way of attempting to dominate, when he became emboldened by the distance of technology. He was, at least in his view, anonymous behind the screen. Brad purposely acted out in a challenging manner he probably would not have exhibited in an on-ground class where interpersonal communications would serve as a larger element in the educational experience.

SUMMARY

The *consumer learner* dialogue continues in *Stories From the Trenches: Lived Experiences of Practitioner Educators in the Contemporary Classroom*. This highly anticipated follow-up to the first collaboration by Dr. Gillian Silver and Dr. Cheryl Lentz gives voice to the authentic experiences of faculty and administrators, along with the relevant perspectives of college and university students. Key elements of the discussion include: evolving attitudes and behaviors that lead to learning environment challenges, poor research skills and over-reliance on poorly constructed user-generated content sites, the urgent need for cultivation of critical thinking acumen, and the importance of equally shared learning community values.

To follow or contribute to the discussion, go to www.consumerlearner.com.

References

Allen, I., & Seaman, J. (2008). *Staying the course: Online education in the United States.* Needgam, MA: Sloan Consortium.

Anheier, H. (2005). *Nonprofit organizations: Theory, management, policy.* New York, NY: Routledge.

Arum R., & Roksa, J. (2011). *Academically adrift: Limited learning on college campuses.* Chicago, IL: University of Chicago Press.

Beder, H. (1989). Purposes and philosophies of adult education in Merriam, S. B. & Caffarella, R.S. (1989). *Handbook of adult and continuing education.* (Eds.). San Francisco, CA: Jossey- Bass Inc.

Brookfield, S. D. (1987). *Developing critical thinkers: Challenging adults to explore alternative ways of thinking and acting.* San Francisco, CA: Jossey-Bass Publishers.

Brookfield, S. (1991). *Understanding and facilitating adult learning.* San Francisco, CA: Jossey-Bass.

Brookfield, S. D. (1992). Developing criteria for formal theory building in adult education. *Adult Education Quarterly, 42*(2), 79–93.

Brookfield, S. (1995). *Becoming a critically reflective teacher.* San Francisco, CA: Jossey-Bass.

Brubacker, J. S., & Rudy, W. (2004). *Higher education in transition: A history of American colleges and universities* (4th ed.). New Brunswick, NJ: Transaction Publishers.

Burge, L. (2008). Crafting the future: Pioneer lessons and concerns for today. *Distance Education 29*(1), 5–17.

Case, P., & Alward, G. (1997). *Patterns of demographic, economic and value change in the Western United States.* A report to the Western Water Policy Review Advisory Commission.

Cameron, K. S., & Quinn, R. E. (2011). *Diagnosing and changing organizational culture: Based on the competing values framework.* (3rd ed.). San Francisco, CA: Jossey-Bass.

Classroom assessment techniques. (2002). Phoenix, AZ: The University of Phoenix Press.

The College Board Policy Center. (2011). Retrieved from http://advocacy.collegeboard.org/

Colvin, J. (2006). *Earn college credit for what you know* (4th ed.). Chicago, IL: CAEL.

CSU-Global. [Producer]. (2010). *Alan Knox: What is meant by learner content and characteristics and how can that information help us be better adult educators.* [Video]. Available from http://csuglobal.blackboard.com

CSU-Global. [Producer]. (2010). *Wlodkowski's four pillars of a cultural responsive teaching model.* [Video]. Available from http://csuglobal.blackboard.com

Dwek, C. S. (1986). Motivational processes affecting learning. *American Psychologist, 41,* 1040–1048.

Dweck, C. S., & Leggett, E.L. (1988). A social-cognitive approach to motivation and personality. *Psychology Review, 95,* 256–273.

Digest for Education Statistics. (2009). *College enrollment and enrollment rates of recent high school completers, by sex: 2000 through 2006.* Retrieved from http://nces.ed.gov/programs/digest/d07/tables/dt07_191.asp

Diversity Graphis.com. (2009). *Teach-Tolerance.* Retrieved from http://www.diversitygraphics.com/Teach-Tolerance-TP?cid=10118

Elliott, E. S., & Dweck, C. S. (1988). Goals: An approach to motivation and achievement. *Journal of Personality and Social Psychology, 54*(1), pp. 5–12.

Fiddler, M., Marienau, C., & Whitaker, U. (2006). *Assessing learning: Standards, principles and procedures.* Chicago, IL: CAEL.

References

Fidishun, D. (2008). *Andragogy and technology: Integrating adult learning Theory as we teach with technology.* Penn State University. Retrieved from http://frank.mtsu.edu/~itconf/proceed00/fidishun.htm

Gamble, J. (2010). *Essentials of strategic management* (2nd ed.). New York, NY: McGraw Hill/Irwin.

Gardner, H. (1983). *Frames of mind: The theory of multiple intelligences* (10th anniversary ed.). New York, NY: Basic Books.

Gardner, H. (1993). *Multiple intelligences.* New York, NY: Basic Books.

Gardner, H. (1995). *Leading minds: An anatomy of leadership.* New York, NY: Basic Books.

Gardner, H. (1999) *Intelligence reframed: Multiple intelligences in the twenty-first century.* New York, NY: Basic Books.

Gardner, H. (2007, March). The ethical mind. *Harvard Business Review,* 51–56.

Goleman, D. (1995). *Emotional intelligence: Why it can matter more than IQ.* New York, NY: Bantam Press.

Goleman, D. (1998). *Working with emotional intelligence.* New York, NY: Bantam Press.

Goleman, D. (2005). *Emotional intelligence: Why it can matter more than IQ* (10th ed.). New York, NY: Bantam Books.

Hames, R. D. (2007). *The five literacies of global leadership: What authentic leaders know and you need to find out.* West Sussex, UK: John Wiley & Sons.

Heidelberg, C. A. I. (2008). Edutainment and convergence: Utilization in higher education from the perspective of entertainment professionals. (Doctoral dissertation). Retrieved from ProQuest Dissertations and Theses database http://search.proquest.com/docview/89202555?account id=35812

Holton, E. F., Knowles, M. S., & Swanson, R. A. (2005). *The adult learner: The definitive classic in adult education and human resource development* (6th ed.). Burlington, NY: Elsevier.

How does it differ from the traditional approach? (2010). *Concept to Classroom.* Retrieved from http://www.thirteen.org/edonline/concept2class/inquiry/index_sub1.html

How students develop online learning skills (2010). *EQ Quarterly*. Retrieved from http://www.educause.edu/EDUCAUSE+Quarterly/EDUCAUSEQuarterlyMagazineVolum/HowStudentsDevelopOnline-Learni/157435

Inside Higher Ed. (2009). *Growing online enrollments, Fall 2002 to Fall 2008*. Retrieved from http://www.insidehighered.com/news/2010/01/27/online

Kickul, G., & Kickul, J. (2006). Closing the gap: Impact of student proactivity and learning goal orientation on e-learning outcomes. *International Journal on E-Learning, 5*(3), 361–372.

Klein, H. J., & Lee, S. (2006). The effects of personality on learning: The mediating role of goal setting. *Human Performance, 19*(1), 43–66.

Knowles, M. S. (1950). *Informal adult education.* New York, NY: Association Press.

Knowles, M. S. (1962). *A history of the adult education movement in the USA.* New York, NY: Krieger.

Knowles, M. S. (1973, 1990). *The adult learner. A neglected species* (4th ed.). Houston, TX: Gulf Publishing.

Knowles, M. S. (1975). *Self-directed learning. A guide for learners and teachers.* Englewood Cliffs, NJ: Prentice Hall/Cambridge.

Knowles, M. S. (1980). *The modern practice of adult education: From andragogy to pedagogy.* Englewood Cliffs, NJ: Cambridge Adult Education.

Knowles, M. S. (1983). *Self-directed learning: A guide for learners and teachers.* Cambridge, MA: Cambridge Book Company.

Knowles, M. S. (1989). *The making of an adult educator. An autobiographical journey.* San Francisco, CA: Jossey-Bass

Knowles, M. S. (1990). *The adult learner: A neglected species.* Houston, TX: A Gulf Publishing Company.

Knowles, M. S., Holton, E. F., & Swanson, R. A. (2005). *The adult learner: The definite classic in adult education and human resource development* (6th ed.). San Diego, CA: Butterworth-Heinemann.

Knox. A. (2009). *Major generalizations about adults as learners are useful to help adults learn and use what they learn? How can educators use such gen-*

References

eralizations? [Video] Available from http://csuglobal.blackboard.com/webapps/portal/frameset.jsp?tab_id=_2_1&url=%2fwebapps%2fblackboard%2fexecute%2flauncher%3ftype%3dCourse%26id%3d_78027_1%26url%3d

Kolb, D. A. (1984). *Experiential learning.* Englewood Cliffs, NJ: Prentice-Hall.

Lentz, C. (2008, 2010). *Journey outside the golden palace: A story of transformation.* Las Vegas, NV: The Lentz Leadership Institute.

Lentz, C. (2009a). *Fail faster: Succeed sooner.* In C. Lentz (Ed.), The refractive Thinker®: An anthology of doctoral writers (Vol. 1. pp. 145–155). Las Vegas, NV: The Refractive Thinker® Press.

Lentz, C. (2009b). *The world according to Dr. Cheryl Lentz.* Retrieved from http:www.drcheryllentz.com

Merriam, S. B., & Caffarella, R. S. (1989). *Handbook of adult and continuing education.* (Eds.). San Francisco, CA: Jossey- Bass Inc.

Merriam, S. B. M., & Caffarella, R.S. (1999). *Learning in adulthood: A comprehensive guide.* San Francisco, CA: Jossey- Bass Inc.

Meyer, K. (2008). If higher education is a right, and distance education is the answer, then who will pay? *Journal of Asynchronous Learning Networks, 12*(1), 45–68.

Miller, G., & Schiffman, S. (2006). ALN business models and the transformation of higher education. *Journal of Asynchronous Learning Networks. 10*(2).

O'Neil, J., & Lamm, S. L. (2000). Working as a learning coach team in action learning. *New Directions for Adult & Continuing Education, 87,* 43–52.

Paul, R., & Elder, L. (2006). *The art of Socratic questioning.* Tomales, CA: The Foundation for Critical Thinking.

Robinson, R. D. (1994). *Helping adults learn and change.* (Rev. ed.). West Bend; WI: Omnibook Co.

Ruch, R. (2003). *Higher Ed, Inc. The rise of the for-profit university.* Baltimore, MD: The John Hopkins University Press.

Sperling, J. (2000). *Rebel with a cause: The entrepreneur who created the uni-*

versity of phoenix and the for-profit revolution in higher education. New York, John Wiley & Sons.

Sperling, J., & Tucker, R. (2005). *For-profit higher education: developing a world-class workforce.* New Brunswick, CT: Transaction Publishers.

Stober, D. R., & Grant, A. M. (Eds.). (2006). *Evidence based coaching handbook.* New York, NY: John Wiley & Sons.

Stubblefield, H., & Keane, P. (1989). The history of adult and continuing education. In Merriam, S. B. & Caffarella, R. S. (1989). *Handbook of adult and continuing education.* (Eds.). San Francisco, CA: Jossey-Bass Inc.

The U.S. Census. (2010). Retrieved from http://2010.census.gov/2010census/

VandeWalle, D., Cron, W. L., & Slocum, J. W. (2001). The role of goal orientation following performance feedback. *Journal of Applied Psychology, 86*(4), 629–640.

Van derWerf, M. (2009). The college of 2020. *Chronicle Research Services. White House: Issues Education.* Retrieved from http://www.whitehouse.gov

Voorhees, R. A., & Lingenfelter, P. E. (2003). *Adult learners and state policy.* Denver, CO: State Higher Education, Council for Adult and Experiential Learning.

Washburn, J. (2005). *University, Inc. The corporate corruption of higher education.* New York, NY: Basic Books.

Walter, T., Knudsvig, G., & Smith, D. (2003). *Critical thinking: Building the basics.* Belmont, CA: Wadsworth Cengage Learning.

Weimer, M. (2002). *Learner-centered teaching: Five key changes to practice.* San Francisco, CA: Jossey-Bass.

Wiggam, M. K. (2004). Predicting adult learner academic persistence: Strength of relationship between age, gender, ethnicity, financial aid, transfer credits, and delivery methods. (Doctoral dissertation, Ohio State University). *Digital abstracts 65*(07), 2460.

Wlodkowski, R. (1998). *Enhancing adult motivation to learn: A comprehensive guide for teaching all adults.* San Francisco, CA: Jossey-Bass, Inc.

Yorks, L. (2000). The emergence of action learning. *Training and Development, 54,* 56.

Index

A

Accountability, 22, 24, 56, 101, 106
Adult learner, definition, 4
Adult learning model, 98
Aging society, 43
Alignment, 10, 34, 52, 68
Alignment of interest, 52
Andragogical, 14, 21, 46, 55, 2, 64, 69, 72, 75, 91
Andragogy, 4, 7, 19, 20, 25, 33, 56, 64, 69
Asynchronous, 61, 65, 72

B

Barriers, adult learning, 8, 24, 68
Base of expectations, 24
Bridge academic theory, 23

C

Community colleges, 9, 11, 102
Consumer driven curriculum, 13
Continuum of dependency, 36
Critical thinking skills, 15, 22, 80, 86

Curriculum integrity, 33
Customer service expectation(s), 6, 46

D

Degree attainment, 59, 99
Distance learning, 33, 63, 64
Divergent needs, 19, 21, 23, 25, 27

E

Educational access, 32
Educational consumption, 32, 41
Educational exchange, 6, 22, 47
Educational transformation, 61
Educational triad, 99
Edutainment, 42, 62, 63
Etymology, 3
Experiential learning, 4, 54

F

Family Education Rights and Privacy Act (FERPA), 70
First generation, 16, 32
Fiscal demands, 15

G
Guided inquiry, 66

H
Hierarchical structure in classroom, 22
Higher Learning Commission (HLC), 55

I
Instructional methodology, 33
Intellectual discourse, 25, 62, 72, 98

L
Lagging indicator, 10

N
Non-traditional learner, 16

O
Online learning, 62, 66–68, 71
Online learning platform, 62

P
Part-time faculty, 51, 52
Philosophical shift, 1

R
Reins of influence, 25
Return on investment (ROI), 47, 49, 58, 80, 99
Rocking chair strategy, 83

S
Satisfaction, 6, 42, 46, 49, 52, 81, 99
Single-gender school, 31
Social compliance, 48
Social experience, 47, 48, 57, 58
Socratic Method, 36
Socratic questioning, 36, 96
Student as consumer, 13
Synchronous, 61, 62, 72
System infrastructure, 61

T
Technology, 4, 01, 13, 33, 43, 61–63, 65, 67–71, 78, 90–92
Transactional business approach, 5, 44
Transferrable skills, 8, 41
Transformation/Transformational, 1–3, 5, 8, 12, 38, 43, 49, 67, 71–73, 83, 95, 97, 100

V
Variance(s), 19, 33, 49, 68
Virtual classroom, 61, 65

W
What's-in-it-for-me (WIFM), 20, 34
Whole learner perspective, 90
Wisdom, conventional, 23, 36, 96, 97, 103

About the Authors

DR. GILLIAN SILVER

Dr. Gillian Silver, ABC, is an accomplished integrated marketing communications and strategic planning professional. Her extensive experience spans corporate-level vice president and director positions for companies with both domestic and international operations, and she has nearly two decades in the higher education arena as a professor at the Bachelor's, Master's, and Doctorate level.

Dr. Silver achieved a Ph.D. in Organizational Leadership, and authored the nation's first study on non profit executive leadership. Further, she holds a Master's degree in Management/Organizational Development, and a Bachelor's in Mass Communications/Journalism, and a Bachelor's of Fine Arts in Theatre.

Earning more than 200 writing, an editing and project/campaign awards, Dr. Silver holds the prestigious Accredited Business Communicator designation from IABC. She was named IABC's "Communicator of the Year," NAWBO's "Woman of Distinction/Marketing," and is a Las Vegas Chamber of Commerce's "Community Achievement/Communications" recipient. Dr. Silver is an inaugural inductee into the Nevada Women's Chamber of Commerce Nevada Women's Hall of Fame. She has been recognized for her competency and student-oriented philosophy with educator excellence awards at the College of Southern Nevada, Maricopa Community College, and University of Phoenix.

Additional published works include her dissertation: *A Qualitative Examination: Ways of Leading Among Non-Profit Executives*, and scores of industry and feature articles.

To reach Dr. Gillian Silver, please e-mail gsilver@strategicresource.com

About the Authors

DR. CHERYL LENTZ

Southern Nevadan author Dr. Cheryl A. Lentz holds several accredited degrees; a Bachelor of Arts (BA) from the University of Illinois, Urbana-Champaign; a Master of Science in International Relations (MSIR) from Troy University; and a Doctorate of Management (DM) in Organizational Leadership from the University of Phoenix School of Advanced Studies.

Dr. Cheryl, affectionately known as 'Doc C' to her students, is a university professor on faculty with Colorado State University-Global, Embry-Riddle University, University of Phoenix, The University of the Rockies, and Walden University. Dr. Cheryl serves as a dissertation committee member, faculty mentor, is a dissertation coach and also offers expertise in editing for APA style for graduate thesis and doctoral dissertations. She has earned her Sloan C Certification from Colorado State University—Global as well as her Quality Matters Peer Reviewer (APP/PRC) Certification.

Dr. Cheryl is also an active member of Alpha Sigma Alpha Sorority.

Additional published works include her dissertation: *Strategic Decision Making in Organizational Performance: A Quantitative Study of Employee Inclusiveness*, *The Golden Palace Theory of Management*, *Journey Outside the Golden Palace*, and the multiple-award-winning *Refractive Thinker* series, Volumes I through VI (www.refractivethinker.com).

To reach Dr. Cheryl Lentz for information on any of these topics, please visit her website: http://drcheryllentz.com or e mail: drcheryllentz@gmail.com

THE NEXT OFFERING FROM THE
Pensiero Press

EFFECTIVE
Study Skills
IN **5** SIMPLE STEPS

Dr. Cheryl Lentz has compiled the valuable information she gives in her blog in one easy-to-use handbook. The study tips are designed to help any student improve learning and understanding, and ultimately earn higher grades. The handbook is not so large that it requires long hours of reading, as is the case with many books on the subject. The information is written in a manner to help a learner "see" and "practice" proven study techniques. Effective study skills must be practiced to for improvement to occur.

PUBLICATIONS ORDER FORM

From The Refractive Thinker® Press:

- ❏ *The Refractive Thinker®: Volume I: An Anthology of Higher Learning*
- ❏ *The Refractive Thinker®: Volume II: Research Methodology*
- ❏ *The Refractive Thinker®: Volume II: Research Methodology, 2nd Edition*
- ❏ *The Refractive Thinker®: Volume III: Change Management*
- ❏ *The Refractive Thinker®: Volume IV: Ethics, Leadership, and Globalization*
- ❏ *The Refractive Thinker®: Volume V: Strategy in Innovation*
- ❏ *The Refractive Thinker®: Volume VI: Post-Secondary Education*

Please contact the Refractive Thinker® Press for book prices, e-book prices, and shipping. Individual e-chapters available by author: $3.95 (plus applicable tax). www.refractivethinker.com

From Pensiero Press:

- ❏ *The Consumer Learner: Emergence and Expectations of a Customer Service Mentality in Post-Secondary Education*
- ❏ *Effective Study Skills in 5 Simple Steps*
- ❏ *Journey Outside the Golden Palace*

Please send more FREE information:

❏ Speaking engagements   ❏ Educational seminars   ❏ Consulting

Join our Mailing List:

Name: _____

Address: _____

City: _____ State: _____ Zip: _____

Telephone: _____ Email: _____

Sales tax: NV Residents please add 8.1% sales tax

Shipping: *Please see our website for shipping rates.*

Please mail or fax form to:

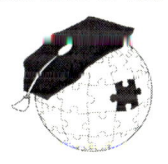

The Refractive Thinker® Press/
  Pensiero Press
9065 Big Plantation Ave.
Las Vegas, NV 89143-5440 USA

CPSIA information can be obtained
at www.ICGtesting.com
Printed in the USA
LVOW11*1534300817
546973LV00010B/281/P